"A fully alive woman writes a fully alive book. Bonnie Danowski delights and inspires with her insights, musings and resilience in courageously living the path that beckoned. I loved reading this book."
—**Michael Morwood**, Author of *Prayers For Progressive Christians* and other titles

"An honest and inspiring love story. This is a journey of living an authentic and spiritual life and truly loving your partner and family in sickness and in health. This will make you laugh and cry. It is tender and honest and touching. I had a hard time putting it down and the poems were a treasure sprinkled throughout."
—**Dana Marie Kennedy, MSW**, Aging Expert/ Advocate

"Bonnie Danowski and I have something in common: multiple sclerosis; I as a patient and Bonnie as a caregiver. Through the illness journey, we've learned about uncertainty in the face of illness, but also about the gifts that come out of managing one. Bonnie's path is filled with reflections and resurrection, and in this book, she immerses herself in both with a combination of autobiography, poetry and prose that demonstrates a full life, with pensive and thoughtful stops along the way. I've been awed by her wisdom from the start and these pages amplify it. I loved reading this book."
—**Kate Milliken**, Founder, MyCounterpane

"As she embarks with open eyes and open heart on the path that never ceases to beckon, Bonnie Danowski reveals, in an engaging, often poetic style, a generous and resilient spirit moving through, and reacting to, a deeply rewarding life shared with loving family and countless friends, though interrupted by her husband's achingly prolonged terminal illness, accompanied at every step by a richly imagined 'Good and Generous God' who supplies her trusting and compassionate soul with guidance, inspiration, confidence and comfort when it is needed."

—**Robert Longoni,** Former Director of the University of Arizona Poetry Center, Author of *Woodpiles*

The Path Beckoned

I Answered Yes

To Laura,
Thank & always in love
& gratitude. Thank you, my
Al-Anon Sister.
Bonnie
5. 7. 2022

The Path Beckoned

I ANSWERED YES

Bonnie Goldsmith Danowski

Poet, Teacher, Caregiver & Advocate

Paper & Seed

Navasota, Texas

Published in the United States of America by Paper & Seed
PO Box 1245, Navasota, TX 77868 USA
www.paperandseed.com

Printed in the United States of America

ISBN 978-1-7332377-7-2 (pbk)

Library of Congress Control Number: 2022905329

Edited by Rebecca Dias (Paper & Seed)

Cover design by Linda Davis and Rebecca Dias

Graphic design by Rebecca Dias (Paper & Seed)

Author bio photo (p. 282 & back cover) by Laura C. Bird, printed by permission, courtesy of Laura C. Bird.

Author photo (p. 115) by Siobhan McCurdy Taylor, printed by permission, courtesy of Siobhan Taylor.

All other photographs, including the photograph used for the cover design, are from the Danowski family collection, printed by permission, courtesy of author.

Scriptures taken from the Holy Bible, New International Version®, NIV®. Copyright © 1973, 1978, 1984, 2011 by Biblica, Inc.™ Used by permission of Zondervan. All rights reserved worldwide. *www.zondervan.com*.

"A Happy Birthday to You, Mom" (p. 47) and "Eulogy for Jim Danowski" (p. 273) by Chris Danowski, printed by permission, courtesy of Chris Danowski.

"Desert Pilgrim" (p. 137) by Jim Danowski, printed by permission of Danowski family, courtesy of author.

10 9 8 7 6 5 3 2 1

For my sons, Mike and Chris—
my life would be empty without you;
for caregiving families;
and for those who spend countless hours
making the world a better place.

CONTENTS

II. CARVED IN SAND & STONE

4. In Praise of Women 69

III. Fog, Light, Sun & Moon

IV. Yes, This Is My Path

ACKNOWLEDGMENTS

I know how blessed I am because of all of the people I want to thank who loved me along the path and gave me the confidence to write this book. I fear in naming you, I would certainly forget someone. I think you'll know who you are. Thank you.

My family of origin, you gave me the solid foundation I needed to live with integrity.

The Danowski family, you loved and welcomed me into your family and taught me true family dedication. My Iowa, Wisconsin, and Arizona friends, you helped me to discover gifts I never knew I had.

The Franciscan Friars, you taught me the way of Francis and Clare of Assisi. I learned compassion and found lifelong confidantes.

Young Christian Workers and Christian Family Movement, I learned that faith is meant to be carried into public life.

Franciscan Renewal Center, who believed in me and empowered so many to walk with the poor and the wealthy.

Contemplative Payer International, National Multiple Sclerosis Society, ARCH Respite Network, National Family Caregivers Association; the national, state, and local boards, committees and organizations I was apart of, you gave me ways to be effective with policymakers and those in power.

Valley Interfaith Project, the "university without walls," who teaches how to be effective in public life. I learned how to bring together people of all faiths, cultures, and social status, to find common interests and change unjust systems. I learned more and accomplished more than I ever could have dreamed of.

In the writing of this book, I wish to acknowledge three specific people who made it possible.

Bob Longoni, you took the first look at my writings and gave me guidance throughout the process of it becoming a manuscript.

Linda Davis, cover designer, you made a work of art from an old photograph.

Rebecca Dias, Paper & Seed, my editor and publisher, you stuck with me, always encouraging, advising, holding me up when I was tired or discouraged and rejoicing when we saw it coming to fruition.

Because of yesterday and all of you, I look forward to tomorrow and all the gifts it will bring.

WELCOME, DEAR READER

Welcome to a life of laughter and tears, mountains and valleys, day and night: my life.

Within everyone lives a story, waiting to be told. It's a story worth discovering and telling. The discovering and telling is for us to do, not only for ourselves, but for our children, grandchildren and all those who will come after us. It dwells in the deepest cavern of our souls. The story is an integral piece of all that was, is, and will be. Dig deep, dear reader, find your story, and claim it as your very own unique tale. Then you will know that it must not be kept within.

This is my story. My hopes are that you find something in these pages that you can use or share with another traveler on this earthly journey. We don't know what is around the next corner. All we know is that there is a next corner, and the adventure of discovering it makes us who we are.

I began writing my story when I was a little girl where rolling hills define the landscape of northeastern Iowa. This fertile land grows tall corn, golden oats, and green alfalfa like none you will ever see anywhere else. It's a place where families work together and grow healthy and strong. No one moves far from home. These are my beginnings. A family of six: Mom, Dad, my three brothers, and me. It was an idyllic childhood, though I didn't know it at the time. Somehow, inside of me, there was a knowing that I would not stay, that there were adventures out there and I was meant to live them.

Four days before my 21st birthday, when this Arizona desert called me, I packed up my 1960 Ford, setting out on the most unpredictable journey I could ever have imagined. It was not the usual path an Iowa farm girl chose in those days. The call must have been stronger than it was sensible. I left my family that morning filled with anticipation and sadness. I guess it was the excitement of new life contrasted with loss of my beginnings, knowing how much I would miss these people I loved so dearly. Why that pull was so strong I don't even try to understand. Yet, today my faith tells me it was to find my best friend and confidant—my life mate.

I'm a woman filled with imaginings, yet a strong pull to reality. I'm a country girl, transported to a city of more than a million. Adapting from the verdant green of Iowa to the brown desert of Arizona was no small feat. It caused so much confusion that I knew I had to write. I thought it important to take all of that chaos in my brain and find some clarity through writing. The "committee" met regularly up there. Seldom did they come to a conclusion that was agreeable to all. You see, I was born under the sign of the Gemini, the twins on the astrological chart. Geminis are of two minds, consistently seeing two sides (and more) to life. I reasoned that if I put the contradicting thoughts on paper, my mind would clear—though I'm not sure that happened. I guess not, since I have filled more pages than I can count, and still, I write.

I have no set style. Whether poetry, prose, story, autobiographical sharing or fictional stories, I just write what seems to be in my head and heart at the time. Readers should note that stories told from the perspective of "I" and "me" are autobiographical, and share my personally lived experiences.

Perhaps the only thing common to my writing is that it comes to me as I put the words to paper. The words do seem to write themselves, and I let them take the lead. Each thought and often the ending is a surprise, even to me. I guess that takes trust. Or perhaps, it is only lack of discipline.

Today I look at my journey with both gratitude and regret. Somehow they live in contrast, but are comfortable with one another. And so it seems fitting to fill in the blanks that make my story mine. I hope you find yours.

I

THE SUN LIGHTS A PATH

I gladly stepped onto the pathway,
only to discover there really was none.
Knowing we never walk alone,
I grabbed hold of the Spirit's hand
and walked on.

CHAPTER 1

Spirit Within

NEVER ALONE

Somehow, somewhere, as a child I learned and believed that no matter what, I would never be all alone. No, I didn't have an imaginary friend—well, maybe I did, but this was different. I didn't understand intellectually, but there was this unnameable "Presence" in my life. That wasn't logical, not explainable. But deep down I knew some being held me, walked with me, and would always be there.

As a teenager raised in the Christian tradition, I identified this presence as Jesus. If I had been born into another tradition, I guess it would have been different. Today I just know it is a Divine Presence, and it doesn't matter what the name is.

My heart recognizes, accepts, and holds this awareness of a constant Presence in my life. This has been paramount in how I go through my days. Oh, I might say and feel at a particular moment that things are dire, ask questions about what do I do now? That's on the surface of my thinking and knowing. If I take the time to ask myself, "What is happening?" and "What am I going to do?"—not easy questions when things look hopeless—this gentle, loving Presence assures me that all is as it is meant to be, that "we" will be ok.

The pieces in this section reflect that as best I can— for now. Once again, my hope is that you, the reader, find a thought that touches the part of you where Your Faithful Presence lives.

I HEAR MY NAME

From the distance I hear my name
In the nearness, I hear my name
Being called by You, my Maker
I hear "I love you, Dear One"

Your voice calls
In the wind, the rain,
The bright sunny day
The deep darkness of the night

I hear my name in the echoes
In the valley, from the mountains
You call me, my Creator,
Always by name

By grace, only grace
Do I hear and answer
I am here, I am here
To do your will.

Teach me your ways
And I will say yes
With my mind
My body, my heart

May I walk as your trusted child
For you have taught me
In the deafening noise of each day
And the welcomed silence

It is in your arms, my God
There is safety and love
And I know that all will be well
Indeed, all shall be well

I do believe,
Help my unbelief

BE PRESENCE

Universal Mystery
Don't let me not recognize You
Within and not remember
My direct connection to You

I breathe You in and out
We are one
I want to be Your presence
To bring what Jesus brought

To be peace, kindness,
Love, hospitality
To be just and unafraid
A Truth searcher and speaker

"Deliver the message,"
You say
"I, your God, am here
Speak My words
To all who will hear."

COME NOW

My beautiful ones
Do not chase rainbows
For their beauty fades quickly

No, look within
There to find in the quiet
The more beautiful

Abide there
In the tent of solitude
Prepared with love

Come now
To the silence

The Spirit chases
Finds and
Prays you

SHHH

Shhh. Listen.
Do you hear?
In the quiet
The stillness
The emptiness

Do you hear?
The Maker is calling
Lovingly waiting
In the quiet
The stillness
The emptiness

Shhh. Listen.
Your heart opens wide
The Maker slips in
Loving your quiet
Embracing your stillness
Filling your emptiness

Shhh. Listen.
In one moment
Your life has changed
You hear
And now you know

Shhh.

Listen.

FOREVER

We are protected, cared for
Loved, nurtured, challenged
We are always of the Creator

Forever tied, forever linked
The created belongs to the Creator
As any work of art to its artist

Though free to go and be wherever
Destiny calls, we remain
The Creator's

To be all we can become
All we are meant to be
All that is possible

Most of all,
To be all that is
Good, good, good,
Good

THAT FEELING

That feeling
You know, that feeling
In the center,
The deep center of your stomach

Gripping,
Consuming
Frightening
Even terrifying

What is it this time?
Where did it come from?
It paralyzes me
I can only cry out "Help"

But what is it?
Do I have to know? No
The Spirit who dwells within
And surrounds all knows

Take a breath
Breathe the Spirit in
Breathe the Fear out
Easier, slower

Stay there
Awhile
All is well

TELL ME WHY

Loving Creator of the Universe
Tell me why
The sun shines so bright
The earth cries for rain
Baby quail escape the nest
Mother and Father call loudly

Babies peep and peep and peep
Running here and there
Little puff balls, little feet
Already the start of plumes
On their tiny heads

Tell me why
Leaving mother and father
Is the plan of the Universe
Babies not always ready
Leave too soon

Go back go back
Before it's too late
Grow bigger, sprout wings
Wings to carry once tiny beings
Skyward to discovery

Tell me why
Being safe is elusive
Out there. Yet—
All of the universe calls:
Grow, learn, be ready

Now it is time
Adventure waits
Leave the nest
Search discover go
Now is the time

HE IS RISEN

Jesus is risen
Dazzling in his resurrection
Death has lost again
And new life begins

The promise of transformation
As he leaves darkness behind
Absorbs and becomes light
For all who can see

A promise that we too
Can walk through death
Absorb and become light
For all who can see

YOU ARE MINE

It is yours to receive
All gift—this gift
Of silence
Of listening

Hear the small whisper
Coming from
Your deepest soul
As it bursts open

A channel leads
To truth and wisdom
The stuff of
Love and eternity

Abide there
Dwell and prosper
In this tent of solitude
Be at home there

You are safe
You are loved
You are free
You are mine

BE

A fleeting message
Here then gone
As life is
As the moment is

Be awake
Don't miss its beauty
Or its ugliness

All we have is now
The last moment gone already
The next yet to come

Live now
It will make a difference
For now
For the next

Be awake
Be grateful
It makes us who we are
For now, for the last, the next

Be true
As true as we can
Sometimes it takes awhile
Sometimes not
We are already forgiven

Be kind
Be like Jesus
Be who we are
Learn that.
It is the best lesson of all

I AM HERE ALWAYS

My faith tells me that the Creator is always faithful, and I think would say, "I am here. I was and always will be."

The Biblical prophets write about this, how God says, I will be your God and you will be my people (Jer. 30.22). Before you were conceived, I knew you (Jer. 1:5). I carved you on the palm of my hand, and when I touched my hand to my heart, you were there (Is. 49:15-16). I love you with a love that never fails. You are in me. I am in your every cell, every minuscule particle—I am the beginning and the end, the Alpha and the Omega (Rev. 22:13).

I am always with you. Do you remember?

When you yelled at your children after a long day and you were late with the rent money; when your mom made you crazy with her all-knowing advice; when the car had a flat and it was 110 degrees and you knew you should have bought new tires (the mechanic had warned you).

When your sister bought that ugly suit and asked you what you thought. When your 8-year-old walked in the door one day and proudly proclaimed, "No more school for me. I know enough." When your best friend just had to be right—and you knew she wasn't.

When your son proudly gave you the crooked shelf that he'd made in Boy Scouts and told you how perfect it would be in the middle of the family room wall. When your granddaughter drew the unplanned—by you, that is—mural of a whale and ocean waves on the bathroom wall—where did she find those waterproof markers?

When your son announced his beloved dog, sporting bowtie and cummerbund, would be best man at his wedding—can he do that? When your daughter decided to deliver your grandchild at home with, horror of horrors, the whole family including her gossipy, bossy mother-in-law there. When your 13-year-old niece confided her excitement at being in love.

When your husband, expressing his youth (yeah, right!) as he turned 50, drove in on a Harley in front of your nosy, smirking nextdoor neighbors.

When your long-time friend needed your strength after her husband left. "Am I going to be okay?" She asked, as you held her close and stroked her cheek.

Yes, I am here—closer to you than you are to yourself. When the sun shines and when the storms come. In the light of day and in the darkest of night. In the pain of illness and in the joy of healing. In the moon and the stars that lead to the morning light. In the emptiness of despair and in the promise of hope. I am here. "I will be your God and you will be my people."

WE COME

Father, we venture into the fields
Sometimes bold, sometimes timid
Sometimes marching, sometimes tiptoeing
Sometimes singing, sometimes crying
Sometimes empowered, sometimes weary
Sometimes self-assured, oftentimes uncertain

But we come, Lord, because of your call
Because of your challenge, your gift
Of faith, your love
Because of your promise
Because you've asked
Because we must

We cannot resist the call
Of parent to child
We are constantly
Drawn back to you who are
Beginning and end

Because you call
We cannot ignore our intrinsic
Longing for completion
Of lover and loved
Creator and created
To be reunited and engulfed in you for always

We come, Lord, to the fields
To do your work

We bring our hands, feet
Bodies, minds, and hearts
Take them and make them yours

CHAPTER 2

The Sea & Other Places

PACK YOUR BAGS

A passport? What do I need that for? Why would I venture past my country's borders? What is out there that I can't find here? The answer elusive for the one who hasn't been there.

The world is a big place. Our worlds are as big or small as our circumstances allow. Many of us don't have the means to travel. Some have so many commitments that being gone for even a day isn't possible. Some are happy with being in one place and staying there. Some travel vicariously through books, other people, movies, documentaries, social media, etc.

I know how fortunate I am to have been able to visit places I used to only read about. I have a passport. I have the ability to go beyond borders that once held me captive. My world is bigger because of the people I've met and places I've been.

I've met people like me and very different from me. I've been enriched by them all. I've seen tiny flowers in the snow on tops of mountains, valleys that held unsolved mysteries, beautiful green fields, the seas that cover most of the earth, underground caverns filled with crystalline beauty. I've seen the artistry of creation in plants and animals, from the tiny cactus to the great redwoods, from the hummingbirds of the air to the whales in the sea. I've heard music and seen paintings, sculptures, theater, and architectural wonders created throughout this beautiful world of ours since the beginning of time. I've met people who spoke languages I didn't understand, who lived in castles, on riverboats, small apartments in large cities, rambling farmhouses, tents, and suburbs where all the houses look the same.

Yes, my world is bigger now; one of the many things I've learned is that everyone and everything is connected in one way or another. I'm grateful for it all.

TAKE ME TO THE OCEAN

Take me to the ocean
Where the cool water washes away
The pain and the loss

Take me to the ocean
Where the roar of the salty waves
Drowns out my lonely cries

Take me to the ocean
Where the sandy beach
Gives life to my bare and tired feet

Take me to the ocean
Where the air
Feeds my pores, my lungs

Where it brings the beats
Of my heart back
Into harmonic cadence

The Maker waits at the ocean
And beckons
Come, my daughter

Be immersed in the life source
Find new life to live, taste,
To hear, see, and feel again

I begin to walk, to run again
To trust again, to love again
Take me to the ocean

Dana Point, CA

ADVENT DREAMS

There was a time
When life was filled with magic
Each day remembered

The magical dreams of the night
Rich with such enticing adventures
Were they real?
Was I carried off by a prince?

Did I fly through the sky on wings of eagles?
Could I see lush valleys
From snow-covered mountaintops?
Did I swim to the bottom of the sea?
Where the fishes come to play?

Grownup adventures
Come from dreams too
Didn't you know?
Take time and believe

See the white dove
Outside the window.
As she drinks from the pond
Fluffing her feathers,

Go with her as she flies
To new wondrous places
Believe in the magic
Of the night as it becomes
The splendor of the day

Take risks, be amazed
It's yours to savor
Be fearless
Taste, touch, see, hear

Advent dreams inspire
Astonishing adventures
Let's go,
Now

BE ALERT

The sea continues its never-ending movement
But calms from the night
Before

The morning comes,
All of creation awakens
Readying itself for what happens today

All called to be alert, no napping
Must not miss a thing
For it is our gift

All of creation is loved
From the starfish who
Washed ashore in the night

To the old man
Who slept last night on the concrete
Bench beneath my window

Both disappeared with the moon
As it descended below the horizon
They'll be back tonight

DUSK SETS IN

Dusk sets in as it does
Predictable, dependable, sure
Each day turns into night
Each week to the next
Each month, year, and on it goes

The waves of the ocean
The tides change
Yet remain the same
Making space
Making room for differences
Diversity, individuality
And the sands shift

We ride the waves
The waves hold the space
Where we become who we are
From dawn to dusk
And thru the darkness of the night

The tides are dependable,
Even predictable
Not so all that occurs
Between each wave
Therein lies the total
Dependence on our God

LONDON

The white fuzzy fog rises
Like smoke from a warming chimney
Covering the Thames, Westminster,
And Big Ben

It comes and it goes
Like thoughts in my mind
Blanketing clarity
Intention and consciousness

I don't like the fog
I cannot see
Into the sky nor into my mind
Lost and lonely

Damp and cold
Isolated
With only memories
Of what was there before

People walk with multicolored umbrellas
Some with only hooded jackets
To stop the rain
But only where they are
In one tiny spot

Some share with another
Newlyweds perhaps
Daughter and father
Son and mother

Husbands and wives
Lovers, all?

Others walk alone
Umbrella or no
Solitary figures disappear
Into the fog

Solitude or chaos?
With no one to talk with
No one to hold
To keep warm with

Look within
The warmth is there, you know
Search for it
Beyond the fog
Within the fog

BEGIN HERE

United Kingdom
Begin here
Homebound but not today
Not tomorrow. One day. Soon
Lost?
Or exploring?
Dark then light

Promised
Believe
Truth
Search now

Heard deep within her soul
Travel on
Echoing through her bones flesh skin
Until completion
Transformation
Wholeness
Ah, begin here

MORNING COMES

At 5 it is warm, dark.
Alone I watch as the darkness
Magically turns to light
Seems but a moment in time

A moment complete
Reconnecting with the source, the sea,
Where life began
Is it also where life will end?
I wonder

As dawn comes, so do the creatures of the air
Come to fly over, to seek their sustenance
From the generous sea waters
That are home to so much life
From the tiny microorganism to the great whale

All designed by,
Created by,
Watched over by,
And intimately loved by
The Creator of All.

I watch as the magnificent pelicans gather
For their morning meal,
Fly, dive, scoop up, and soar away
Others float on the sea, waiting, watching,
For a signal to dive and find the food
That will carry them on
To other near or far-distant waters

Oh, how wonderful the Eternal One
Infinite all-encompassing love
Forever giving and delighting in it all

How blessed the entirety of creation
All a piece of the portrait of the Eternal One
Yet each a complete portrait
A single daisy, prairie dog, butterfly
The fullness of the Eternal

Will life end here?
Still I wonder

THE CONSTANCY OF THE SEA

The waves come
Morning, afternoon
Day and night

The waves come in
They go out
Always predictable

From the beginning of time
No change, no change
No change

God's love—always
There, always here
Always, always

No change no stopping
No newness—even—
Just constant

TRAIN RIDES

On a train from Wengen, Lauterbrunnen,
Interlaken Ost, to Bern, Zurich and Vienna
As we leave this spot, we travel north and east
To our next resting place

Riding the train is scary
Do we have the right ticket
A ticket any ticket
No, that is your timetable

Travel jitters twitches,
The Swiss are accustomed to tourists
Making mistakes
Always, though, given the chance to correct it
More francs, please. Thank you. Merci

Clouds block the sun
Costs too much to be in fog and rain
Why, Spirit, why no sunshine
No spectacular views

Only to look within
There to find the more beautiful
Mountains, waterfalls, valleys
Spirit stuff Divine
The gift of silence
And listening

Listen for the small whisper
Coming from the deepest

Bottom of your soul
Truth takes up its home there
To be drawn on when called

Open that channel to spirit
To truth and wisdom
All is of love and eternity

The train ride
Is like being in a moving picture
Who can sleep and feel justified
I cannot

WAVES

The waves are teeming with
The life of the sea
From whom all life has come

It is good to return to the sea
To return to our beginning place
To know where we have come from
To know where we are going

Oh, but the road is a rich one
That we all must walk
From sea to desert to mountain
To valley to sea

Travel well, the Goddess
Tells her children
Return to me
Travel well

CHAPTER 3

People I've Loved

WALK WITH ME AWHILE

Walk with me awhile and meet some of the people who have been part of my life. Paths are never straight and smooth or lighted well. Maybe that is because we aren't meant to walk alone, we are meant to help and be helped. Sometimes I do believe that our work here is to take hold of the hands of others as we travel on to that place where we began. Of those I've met, some walked with me for a short way, others a long way. Some were shadows that blocked the sun or the moon from view. Each was important enough to me at the time to put what I was thinking and feeling on paper.

MY BEST FRIEND

I have this friend who likes me for me. You know, that's pretty cool. Doesn't expect me to be anyone or anything else. She makes me laugh, like when we're in a clothing store and she goes into the dressing room, and after a couple of minutes yells, "There's no toilet paper in here!" Or she goes into the automotive store and practices her Madonna look using different size funnels. She makes me cry when her husband doesn't appreciate her. She lets me be a little off-center when I do goofy things, like the day I had on one black and one brown shoe. It could have been worse—red and white—I think she was embarrassed that day though. She lets me hold her when she misses her mom. Her mom died last year.

How'd it happen that we became friends? Maybe we were sisters in a past life, or our souls knew each other before God found bodies for them. I don't know for sure. Yeah, you could say she's my best friend, my soul sister. Gift, it's all about gift. Thanks, God, for this most precious gift.

A HAPPY BIRTHDAY TO YOU, MOM!

Written by my son Chris Danowski as a birthday gift to me

Walking through the streets of Paris
On a day as hot as the desert
And we're thinking about art and history
And wishing something were open

There are a hundred coffee shops
All over Europe
Where we stopped to talk about
What we were thinking about
Art and history
And the way things repeat and return

And the time I dragged you and Elli
To look at Kafka's grave on a Sunday morning
It was after we'd seen the Duomo
Appear out of nowhere

Before the Sagrada Familia
We hadn't been there yet
That was another place though
Another time though

So many cathedrals
And so many museums
And they all tend to melt together
All at once

I can't remember which I saw first
I know they speak to each other
But in all these things
The before and after doesn't really mean anything

They are there before and after us
And all at the same time

So, when Elli wants to talk
About the matter of lives mattering
She says activism is
Born into her bones

And I look at her mom
And I look at my mom
(Change is a matrilineal matter)
And I don't wonder where
It all comes from

This is when it makes sense
Why when it's the three of us
Looking at pretty lights
Or why when it's us
Tramping over
Irish cemetery soil
It all makes sense

Her roots are not from me
But ones I got from you
The ones that moved through me
And passed along to her

Because that's how this works
The best things that we have to give
Were the same ones that were given to us
The matter that matters does not belong to us
But to the ones who are not even born yet

Happy birthday, Mom!
I love you,
Chris

Bonnie in Europe

MY TEACHER, MY FRIEND

Have you ever met someone
That you know you've known?
From where, when?
Maybe before your souls
Entered these bodies?

These times, recalled,
Like reunions unexplained
I remember clearly
One time it happened to me

I walked past a man
A twitch of recognition
His first look, a curious one
Do I know you?

Wearing the brown robe
Of the Franciscan Order
A gentle man, a quiet man
Spirit of the warrior
and the peacemaker

A man of deep spirituality
Contemplative, mystic, teacher,
Mentor, even agitator, he
Taught, inspired, empowered

As our friendship grew,
We became partners
At this place of abundance

Where there was so much

So much to give to those
Who had little—
And to those with a lot
From the one on the street
To the one in high places

As Francis met the leper
And the Sultan
We went to darkened streets
And to the US Capitol

From the powerless
To the powerful
Two different worlds
Could we all meet as equals?

Bible in one hand,
Fact sheet in the other
We talked and taught
And made changes

This Friar, my friend
Always there, always prodding
Saying we can do this
Saying we had to do this

This humble man in the brown robe
Stands in the shadow of his God
With a simple but profound message
Do good and avoid evil

Simple, such simple words
Look into his eyes and know
There dwells the Divine
Waiting, just waiting

Stay awhile, do not be afraid
Suddenly it happens
The Divine recognizes the Divine

Now I remember you.
Yes, and I remember you.

A gentle smile says it all

MEET MY FRIEND

My life is filled with gifts, with challenges, with faith, hope and love. Gifts aplenty. Today I'm thinking of this very special gift: My dear, wise friend who is always there, who listens when I'm serious and makes me laugh when I can't find the humor in things.

My friend's sight is diminishing. He may lose his ability to see completely.

I've heard it said when one of our senses is gone, others become stronger. Is that so? For this man, who is husband to Ann, father, grandfather, great-grandfather and my friend, I pray his sense of presence increases. That he hears those little things not heard now. That he will feel even more how much he is loved by so many. That he continues to know what only the gifted ones know.

For today my heart hurts, I am sad. I'm happy that his feelings don't have to be as mine. He is a warrior and will accept with open arms whatever comes his way.

He says if he does lose his sight completely, he will always remember how I look today. I will be an eternal 77.

I want him to see me as I age, as the wrinkles grow deeper, my eyes lose some of their color, my back hurts more and maybe I'll limp. I have this tremor that might get worse.

My hair is already nearly white, someday it will be pure white. He won't see it. I'll be there for him—especially when he doesn't see me coming, and he'll laugh at the surprise!

I know new gifts wait for him. I know his ability to love, to understand, to believe, to find the beauty of all that is, will be enhanced. His true essence will remain. He is a genuine reflection of his Creator. That cannot change. It is the core, the tiny speck, the extraordinary center of all he is. Meet my friend, Mike.

Mike died today. He won't know me as I age. I won't know him when his eyesight is gone. He sees clearly now. I am aging. And we will meet again.

MAGGIE

Wife, mother, grandmother
And so much more
Most of all, child of God
Woman of faith, love, hope
And wisdom

As your eyes meet hers
You see into her soul
She doesn't mind,
In fact, invites you in
Welcome, she says

If you know her
Blessed are you
You have met
A truly anointed one
God's own daughter

The world is better
Because she is here
I'm better
Because she is here.
Thank you, dear friend,
Thank you, God

THIS MAN

Who is this man
From the heartland
Where the corn grows tall,
The air is clear,
The nights alight with fireflies

The West beckoned this young man
To leave behind those he loved
And travel many miles
Following his God, his heart
Within the Order of Franciscans Minor

Destined to serve
Those living on the edge
The poor, the immigrant, the orphan.
Humble, loving, compassionate, this man
Loyal, salt of the earth, genuine

Adventurer, pilgrim, Friar
Lover and Follower of Francis
Who is this man?
His name is Tom
He is my friend

THREE FRIENDS

We came together once again
From different lives
To renew these friendships
So special, so full of grace

Filled with gratitude and wonder
Returning to the seashore
As we had for years

The waves beat on the shore
As we walked in rhythm
And knew all of creation
Reached out in praise to our loving God

As the ocean breezes gently brushed
Our faces, we knew God was
Refreshing our souls

Goodbyes follow hellos
We knew the pain of separation
And were reminded again
Of the imperfections of this life

We held each other tightly
As we recalled our days together
And knew we were already
Transformed

We stepped off the world
It was different this time

As it was each time
It was the same as it was each time

Celebrating in our diversity
And delighting in these friendships
We felt God's touch as the masterpiece
Of our time ended

We each would go a different way
And carry the other with us
Food for the journey
Until next year

FAREWELL FOR NOW

For my dear Australian friends

Australia, land of the outback, koala,
Aborigine, coral reef, and our friends
Michael and Maria from Down Under
Yeahhh, mate!

Outlanders now, once insiders
Michael, man of integrity,
Dreamer, searcher, teacher, lover
Maria, woman of integrity,
Dreamer, searcher, teacher, lover

Today we wish you Bon Voyage,
Go with the love you have gathered here
We send a part of us with you
And a part of you remains with us

All the ground we stand on
Is now blessed, holy, beloved
Because we have loved
Always a part of one another

Travel on, dear friends,
The journeys continue
A little easier now
A little less burdensome

Much more certainty
Rocks on the path

Smoother now
Walk on

Spread the good news
We are one
We will meet again
Yeahhh, mate!

WILL WE TALK AGAIN?

My little brother is dying
As we ended our call last night he asked
"Will we talk again?"

He asked me to listen
To his favorite song
Andrea Bocelli's "Time to Say Goodbye"
I've listened throughout the night
And again this morning

We will talk again.
Maybe by phone
Maybe after he passes through
The thin veil
To a transformed life
Where there is no pain

Fly, little brother, fly
With the angels
Far above and beyond
Anything our human minds
Can understand

There are no words
Only love that transcends
All differences, distance, death
Yes, even death

Death is that gate
We all will pass through

Leading to eternity
When it is time
To go on

Leaving those we know here
Joining those who have gone before.
As we say bon voyage,
Welcome home, Bill, they will say
Free from your broken tired body
And now you know

Until we meet again
Yes, we will talk again
I love you.

IT IS DONE

Today your life is celebrated
You have left us
And moved on
To a place we don't know

You have journeyed on
Continuing the life begun here
With a new understanding
Of what was and what is now

Rest, brother of mine,
But not too long
Be in touch
Love us from where you are

Reach through the veil
And touch those who loved you
And were loved in return
The young, the old, all

Thank you for being my brother.
I love you

A MOMENT OF GRACE & AWE

I remember one time when I was facilitating a bereavement group for widows and widowers. It exemplified what had happened many times within the walls of this space, a space graced by the sharings of the people who came there.

That day there were sixteen people in the group, a hefty number to facilitate discussion. The topic was "Living Alone," and, as usual, we had gotten through only two of the eight tips in the resource I was using.

This was only the third time this man had come. His wife had died 4 months earlier in his arms as he was giving her CPR. He had been working hard to understand the grief that he was experiencing and asked some very hard questions. He was a retired Lt. Col. Special Forces Unit. He was of European, Cherokee and African descent, and a charming, intelligent, handsome, thoughtful man.

Toward the end of our meeting time, he raised his hand and asked if he could say something. Not a timid man, he often asked questions, made comments, asked for advice from the group and was genuinely searching for answers. I said, of course. And with tears in his eyes, this is what he said, "I have been through three wars, I have seen hundreds of people killed. I have killed hundreds of people. Could someone tell me why this death hurts so much?"

I knew this was the first time he'd spoken those words. He didn't really need an answer. The group, however, having also lost beloved spouses, responded quickly with she was his partner, his wife and lover. In his deep grief, he had not been able to recognize that difference between her death and the faceless others killed in combat.

As his tears slowly dried, I saw clearly the veil over his face lifting. He didn't need advice. He just needed a safe place where he could speak the words out loud.

The healing had begun.

II

CARVED IN
SAND & STONE

*How far must we go
to find we have come home
to a place we never left?*

CHAPTER 4

In Praise of Women

WHAT IF?

What if while growing inside of your mother, she had gently rocked you, sung sweet songs of love, hope and faith, and told you sacred stories of the strong women who had gone before you?

What if on the day that you were born, you had been surrounded by your grandmothers, your aunts and your sisters? And as you emerged from the comfortable warmth of your mother, the candlelit room was filled with the peacefulness of precious perfumes and lovely music?

What if after your birth, you were passed from woman to woman as they laughed and talked of other remembered births? They covered you with fragrant, warm oils and lovingly wrapped you in softness before returning you to your mother for your first taste of milk?

What if the day you first went off to school, the women who cherished you had gathered to bless your new beginnings and set you free into the larger world?

What if you had been helped to discover and believe in the ancient spring of energy and life, that was waiting within you to be reclaimed and released?

What if the moment you began to bleed, you were honored, given a new name and ritually welcomed into the holy circle of knowledge and wisdom that would sustain and steady you as you grew into the woman God meant you to be?

What if as you became a mature woman, your teachers had taught you that the gifts that were uniquely yours would help to bring God's justice and harmony to the world?

What if on your wedding day, your foremothers had tenderly bathed, anointed, dressed and prepared you as you walked in beauty and grace toward your new life?

What if when your first child leapt from your womb and entered the world, you had been cared for confidently but gently as you held your newborn baby?

What if as you entered midlife and menopause, your soul sisters had knowingly reassured and reverenced your age and wisdom?

What if when your own granddaughter was born, with awe you had held her, whispered women's ageless secrets, and dreamed timeless dreams with her?

What if when your life is through, all of the faithful women who have loved you surround you with the strength of the ages and softly hold you, bless, laugh and cry with you. They walk with you as they prayerfully send you on your way to that final beckoning door. Filled and fortified from the rich reservoir of those friendships, you travel on alone into the loving embrace of the Creator and all of those who anxiously await your homecoming.

DEANNA'S BABY SHOWER

Welcome, Baby Sister! We have been waiting for you. My wish for you is compassion. As a symbol of that I give to you a stuffed toy, a blue dog. A sister, Pam, gave me a blue dog about a year ago to bring me comfort during a painful time. My wish for you, Little One, is to look at your blue dog and hold her gently as you would those who are hurting or who have hurt you. Let your arms surround her and you will feel God's arms surrounding you. You will find comfort there. We are all a part of one another and of the God who loved us into being. To be compassionate, you must believe in your uniqueness and the uniqueness of all of God's creatures. May you find the joy and peace that are yours when you act out of a compassionate heart.

CAN YOU SEE ME?

When did it happen? When was the first time I noticed that maybe I was invisible? Was it when I was a chubby little girl and no one seemed to notice me—except for the times when I would be teased for not being a cute-tiny-little-thing? That wasn't fair. Or was it when I was in second grade with my cousin, who was a cute-tiny-little-thing? She played the piano better than I did, too. I didn't want to play that dumb thing, anyway. I just wanted to play ball or make-believe with my dolls. Or run around the farm with my big brother and hide from our little brother. I just wanted to make the coaster wagon—that's what we called those little red wagons that every kid had—into a carriage, take a rope and tie it to the horse who then pulled us down the road. One day the wheels fell off, and our butts were dragging on the ground. That took care of that wagon. The wheels probably fell off because I was too big, huh?

I found my visibility, though, in later years in grade school and then in high school. How, you ask? Well, first of all, I slimmed down a bit. I went to three different schools by fourth grade. Considered the new kid at first, I soon discovered I was a natural, born leader who could buck the existing clique. So through the rest of grade school and high school I became visible, as prom queen and all that.

I went to a small junior college where everyone else pretty much knew each other, so, once again as the new kid, I found my visibility in theater. I loved it, and snagged one of the cutest guys on campus—for a year.

Then it was off to the university and back to invisibility. I was running as fast as I could to keep up with chemistry, English literature and algebra. I didn't know, though, I'd run into the cute-tiny-little-things again. I thought I'd gotten rid of them back in second grade. But, no, universities attract cute-tiny-little-things too, you know, and cute-tiny-little-things attract gorgeous big hunks. Back to invisibility. And trauma within my psyche. I walked that huge campus—10 miles per day, they figured. You could tell the difference on the first day of school by looking at the calves of the girls. The upper class girls had legs of steel. It didn't take long for all of us to have these incredible legs— even we big girls. After all, we were carrying around extra weight so that made our legs even stronger. Invisible girls get through school too though. I went and got myself engaged. I was no longer invisible. Soon though I realized I wasn't in love and called off the engagement. It would have been easier if I'd been invisible. I left my family, friends and home to begin a new life in Phoenix.

I found myself the new kid on the block again, smarter but still naïve. In my new job, my boss's personality took over a room. As his assistant, I was invisible—again! Well, that was expected, wasn't it? I did what I could to find my place in this new city, often fearing invisibility. Funny, though, the mirror still told me that I was there. It smiled, scowled, winked back at me.

I went and got myself engaged again. This time it stuck. My visibility was no longer as an individual but as half of a couple. Funny how that happened too.

Where did I go? I became invisible to myself at that point. Seeing myself only as "wife," even though my new husband, Jim, saw me as friend and lover.

Soon I was pregnant and was very visible again, but not as me. I was visible as a carrier of a baby. And, of course, you all know what happened—the visible part of me was my belly. Tell me, would you, why is it that no one would think of patting your stomach under normal circumstances, but when there's a baby in there, the whole world thinks it's their playground— touch the tummy, watch the baby move, get a load of that belly button!

Birthing—a return to visibility. How was I feeling? How are the contractions? You're dilated 7, not much further. Okay, girl, we're ready to go! Some pushes and there he is. Look at the beautiful little boy. To recovery and then to my room. Let me see the baby. Let me hold him—oh, how sweet.

From then on, motherhood took over through two sons, and, you know, this is the time of incredible invisibility. Drive the kids here, drive them there. Go to the little league game, to the soccer game, to drama lessons. Take me to Dan's house, fix my bike, my ear hurts, I have a toothache. Family dinner—that's a must. Focus on how the kids' days were, and ask, "Honey, how was your day at work?"

I just provide the infrastructure around here. That's not important, and no one notices anyway. Clothes are clean and in the drawers, beds are made. I shoveled out the house today, did you notice? And, the new puppy that the kids said they'd groom and clean up after— well, you know that one! Wiping up urine, spraying the carpet, vacuuming up hair. Yeah, sure, this dog won't shed! Mom'll do it.

Don't get sick, that's when you're really invisible because no one wants to admit Mom's sick—it means they have to do what you do. So what do they do? Order out, pick up a pizza. The house? Of course, it's not dirty. Mommmmm! Where's my blue shirt? Honey, can you iron just this one shirt for me—I have an important meeting with a new client today.

Our life was humming along, all the usual happenings in a family of four. We weren't prepared for what came next. It was undoubtedly the most drastic turn our life would ever take.

One day Jim came home from work at 10 am. We knew that wasn't right. To make this short, he spent ten weeks in a hospital and was released with a diagnosis of Multiple Sclerosis. I then truly became the invisible spouse. How's Jim? Look at that young guy in the wheelchair! Nevermind the young woman pushing him and dragging two little boys along. I got lost in the mélange of a whole new way of living. I was the supporting partner. The important person was Jim.

Okay, we learned to live in the new normal. Life is good, really, we jumped another hurdle, laughter returned, love deepened. I looked in the mirror again. Maybe I shouldn't have—my first white hair. My husband didn't even notice. Oh, man, I know what's coming now. I'm gonna turn into a colorless, wrinkled, gray-haired old person. Invisible again, I had better take advantage of the time I have left before the whole world doesn't see me anymore. It helps that the kids are growing up. By golly, they've even learned to—though not without a lot of whining—clean their own rooms, their bathroom, and wash their own clothes, no ironing though. No one does that anymore, anyway. So no bother.

So it was back to school to find the new me. If I hadn't realized I was invisible before, I certainly did then. Here were all of these cute-tiny-little-things, now *young* cute-tiny-little-things, and then there was me—gray—but not for long. I found the hair color aisle in the closest Walgreens and, presto, I was a brunette again. Didn't help much. No one paid a lot of attention to a 40-year-old woman—not even the instructors.

I returned to work with other women whom I had met in the hair color aisle. I was seen again and had become one of the middle-aged workforce. That worked. Except when I was in meetings with men. Have you ever noticed how women can say something and no one hears it, sometimes not even the other women in the group, but five minutes later some guy says the same thing, and everyone goes, "Wow, what a great idea!" Sometimes I would say, "Hey, didn't I just say that?" That too fell on deaf ears, so maybe I didn't say it. Maybe I only thought I had said it. Was the invisibility in my head too? Had they convinced me that I really wasn't there? The mirror said I was.

My work led me directly into public life. I was visible again! I began programs bringing awareness of healthcare needs of the most vulnerable, homelessness, undocumented immigrants, racial injustice, environmental equity, and the dangers of nuclear weaponry. As my career developed, I found my passion: improve the lives of caregivers. Jim's Multiple Sclerosis made it personal for me. There were thousands like me out there, but we were the invisible ones. I was determined to make us visible.

I went from the city council to the Arizona Legislature, governor and our nation's capitol. Being Advocacy Co-Chair of the Arizona Chapter of the National Multiple Sclerosis Society took me to Washington D.C. every spring. People from across the country came together and met with our congressional members with requests for help for our MS families. It became routine to meet with lawmakers and persuade them to help caregiving families. As a founding co-chair of Valley Interfaith Project, I joined others at our state legislature in a successful campaign to establish a Lifespan Respite Care Program resulting in needed support for Arizona's caregiving families.

I stepped out of this highly visible role and back home when Jim required more care. Another step into invisibility. Maybe letting my hair go gray added to that, but it really became a pain to keep coloring it, and then there was that cancer scare too. Probably, though, it was because I was just too lazy and cheap to continue doing my hair.

Then the biggest challenge of all—*menopause!* And why the heck do they call it that, anyway? Men-o-pause. What? Men have nothing to do with it. So, why don't we call it womenopause? And what's the pause all about? A pause is when something stops and then begins again. Like when you're watching a DVD and you need to go to the bathroom, you hit pause. But menopause doesn't stop. It's as if someone came in the middle of the night and stole "me" away from me. You women reading this know. If you don't, you will.

Wrinkles and dry skin—industrial strength lotions. And where the heck did my fanny go? I think it migrated 180 degrees to my front. Gray hair which wouldn't be so bad but it turns yellow. And that purple shampoo! If you leave it on two minutes too long, now your hair is blue! Yes, blue!

Speaking of hair, why is it popping up where it hasn't grown before? And what's with my arms having sprouted wings? My feet hurt, and coffee no longer wakes me up in the middle of the afternoon. Memory. What did I just say? Bifocals. I can't read the label on the low-cal, low-carb energy bar that I've traded in my Mars bar for.

Menopause: no men, no pause—just "O." O, I forgot. O, I didn't mean to do that. O, darn! Or something like that!! O, let's go to the beach. O, I'm tired. O well. O no. O yeahhhhh. O, don't you see me? Once it finally soaks in, menopause, though it's still a ridiculous word, is here to stay. I just wish someone had warned me... time to take control and become visible.

The mirror said I was still there, though I'd forgotten to look for awhile. Now the new me in the mirror is wrinkled, has white hair—wait, there are lines there that show wisdom, that show joy and faith and love. There is hope in my eyes and a smile on my face.

I am not invisible. I will not let the world treat me that way anymore. Here I am, yes, a different version of the 17-year-old prom queen, but still the same smart, talented, creative and attractive woman.

And as far as I am concerned, I don't care what they think. I am beautiful.

OVER THE YEARS WITH MY GRANDDAUGHTER

July 4, 1999, one month before your birth. To my granddaughter as you wait to be born:

You are a very busy little girl these days as you continue to grow inside your mommy, getting ready for your entrance into this world.

I have a couple of things that I want to remind you of, so please give your grandmother a few moments. First—but you do already know this having been around them for 8 months now—you have parents who are totally unique and outstanding. You are in for a wonderful, exciting, searching journey. They will love you, challenge you to be all that you can be (and then some) and give you opportunities to experience life to its full. They will share their relationship with their God with you. Listen carefully, allow your spirit to soar and to find your own place with the Creator who loves us all into being.

I'm hoping that you grow into the realization of your connectedness to your aunts and uncles, grandparents, great-grandparents, cousins—all of these people we call family. With that comes the love we all have for you, the hopes and dreams we have for you, the collective wisdom and joys and sadness that have made us all who we are. May you live life to the full.

You will come across people, too, who are struggling with who they are and aren't ready to be a part of your life. Let them be and don't fret.

Oh, don't forget to spend time with the non-humans, God's other creatures—dogs, they're especially loyal; cats, they're self-sufficient; birds, allow them their freedom; bunnies, so soft and cuddly; fish, who remain tied to the water, source of life; lizards, snakes, bugs, butterflies, worms—they all will teach you something.

Smell the roses, taste the clover, walk on the grass, hug the trees and sit on their branches. Pick tomatoes, pull carrots from the earth, peel oranges fresh from the tree.

Relish every moment. Life goes by too quickly. Love who you are and who you are becoming. Yawn, cry, question, sigh, most of all, laugh. Be happy and never ever forget to thank God for each moment of each day, for it truly is gift. Yes, all of it.

Already you are loved,
Signed: Your Grandmother

Spring has come
New life everywhere
Baby burros
Colts, calves, lambs, children

And a child has come to visit
"Hieeh!" She squeals
With total excitement
And anticipation

As the spring brings the breath

Of future surprises,
So too this little girl,
Bright eyes and sweet smile,
Awaits life's next treat

God smiles—giggles in delight—
At the antics of Her Promised Little One
While the whole earth anxiously longs
For her happy touch

∞

    She came to visit the first time when she was 4 months old. It was Christmas here in the desert, and she came from the cold northern plains. She would curl up in my arms and smile as I talked with her, yes with her, her response fully recognizable in her upturned mouth, or her confused brow, or her sleep-filled eyes.
    Her name is Eliana Abeni. The Hebrew name, Eliana, translates to "God has answered." Abeni is a Yoruba name. It translates to "We asked for her, and behold! She is ours." She's my granddaughter.
    It was during that very first visit that she and I got to know the night sky. It would be in the early evening that we would venture out to look up at the sparkling new stars of winter and the bright white December moon. It was on those nights when she would squirm in my arms as I carried her and showed her the various constellations. And she would look at the beauty all around her, and then look into my eyes as if to say, "Okay, Nana, now let's get to why we're here together," and then I would sing, "When You Wish Upon a Star."

And she would calm, lay her head on my breast and just look and listen. Somehow she knew those millions and millions of brilliant lights formed an incredible tapestry of God's love and promise.

On special nights we would find the North Star and I'd tell her the Christmas story. I would tell her how another baby 2000 years ago surprised his mother and father, just as she had. They hadn't expected to be parents. Neither had Mary and Joseph. I told her I wondered if Jesus had looked down and said to the Creator, "There! There! They are the ones. I want to be their child. It is in their home that I can grow and learn and become all that I am meant to be." And God the Creator said, "So be it. You will bring to the world a new song, a new way. You will grow in awareness throughout your life and will find love, feel sadness, face the unconquerable enemy, and follow your heart. I will be here for you—just look to the sky and find my love and promise in the stars. I love you, my son, I love this world. I made it for you. You will be both fully human and fully God. You'll grow into knowing who you are and what you are to do. You go now and take the good news. Live so that all will know that I am a God of love and justice and peace. But most of all, I am a faithful God. And I will always be so."

And I would tell Eliana that before she was born, her little soul looked down and said, "There! There! They are the ones I want to be my mommy and daddy. God, let me be their child." And God answered, "So be it." Once again, God's gift of life was realized in our midst. And I would tell her that each new life that comes to our earth is a promise of God's faithfulness and love, just as Jesus was.

Over the years this scene has been repeated countless times, though now she comes oftener and she's 9 years bigger than she was that first Christmas. Now we walk hand in hand or sit in the grass and look at God's mantle of stars and listen. And we can almost hear the stars themselves singing, "When You Wish Upon a Star."

Dear Elli, today you are 21. If I could have chosen a granddaughter, I would have chosen you. You came into the world, landed in this family and blessed us in so many ways. Like the orchid, you are lovely, enduring, changing. You are a beautiful young woman with a future filled with dreams built on the firm ground of yesterday's and today's experiences.

I'm sure your dreams are many. Never forget to dream dreams. They are the seeds that sprout and grow into who you will become. Some of those dreams will come true, some will disappear in the blink of an eye, others will be adapted as life happens. Our dreams are the stuff of future miracles. No matter what, be true to yourself, never stop dreaming.

DOES THE GODDESS KNOW

The Goddess knows
Why this has happened
To Her daughter

She sees and smiles Her
Approval that Her daughter
Has allowed herself to feel again

Life is best when lived to the full
She tells her:
Experience the gifts I send you

Let yourself know all there is
Fly with the angels, swim with mermaids
Walk close to the edge

Don't be safe, it's no way to live
No risks, no challenges
No change, no growth

Eat banana splits
Ride motorcycles
Dance sambas

Become all you can be
Don't cheat the Goddess
Or the world or yourself

Stay true to the Goddess
Deep within your soul

Then give it back to Her and to the world
It will bring you happiness
Like you have never
Known

THANKSGIVING PRAYER FOR GINNY

Written for my friend Ginny on her 40th birthday

Creator of Compassion and Courage, the first image of your spirit in scripture is a feminine image. Your "Ruah" hovers over the primeval chaos and brings forth creation. Like a mother bird hovering over her young, so your spirit enfolds her wings over us, protecting us and bringing forth a new creation from our chaotic lives. We are here today in the midst of your wondrous creation, to praise you, to celebrate your image in this beautiful woman, who I am humbled to call my friend, to acknowledge and affirm her life, to dream wonderful dreams, and to dance with delight in what you have done and continue to do in her and through her. We come in your name, Love, Beloved, and Lover.

Bless this time we have together, as we are confident that you always do. We come as wanderers, pilgrims, searchers, faithful servants, who sometimes have successes, sometime make mistakes. And always, we know that you are here beside us, over us, under us, within us. And that tells us that we are yours from before time and well after time is no longer.

Especially today as we celebrate this milestone in Ginny's life, we give you great praise and thanksgiving for all that is, all that has been and all that is to come. You have given our world an incredible gift in this woman. Forty is an awesome time, a time when wisdom becomes more than a concept, when growth becomes a bit more comfortable, direction clearer, and patience a little more understandable. Give her your continuing guidance so she is always aware of being connected to you. Empower her to deeply realize her role as your co-creator. Give her clarity in her womanhood and the gifts that are part of that: her spirituality, sexuality, artistry, gentleness, curiosity, commitedness, who she is as friend, wife, and mother, daughter and sister. She is teacher, leader, confidante, artist, creator, priest, counselor, and lover. And most of all she is your beloved child.

Thank you, Good and Generous God, for our finding each other. As the days, months and years go by, may we find within our own souls the sacred ways that we can be and walk with each other.

Bless her each and every moment of her life with your bounteous love.

Amen.

WAYS OF WISDOM

Written for my women's circle on a weekend trip to Flagstaff, Arizona

Wisdom in Greek translates to Sophia. It is in Proverbs in the Bible Old Testament that we read about Sophia. She is the personification of the female aspects of God. This reflection was shared with my own circle of women when we took a weekend away.

When we have made every effort to understand and we are ready to take upon ourselves the mystery of things; then the most trivial of happenings are touched by wonder, and there may come to us, by grace, a moment of unclouded vision.

Sophia, Wisdom, come. Bring us closer to the very meaning of life. We have followed many routes to happiness, feasted at countless tables in an effort to still our hungers, placed numerous objects at the center of our lives. Yet, we find the gifts of the spirit within: wisdom, compassion, perception. As women of wisdom, we return at last to the truth of our being, the ultimate mystery of the universe, the sacred dimension of existence.

Sophia, teach us, as you do, to speak in the busiest parts of the ancient city, raising our voice in the public square where power is exercised, offering your message to all who will listen. May we experience the sacred through attention, awareness, centering, imagination, action, and paradoxically, darkness. You offer wisdom as God's gift, bringing true knowledge, prudence and discernment. You promise that when we attend to the divine message, we will find joy and delight.

"Blessed are those who find wisdom, those who gain understanding, for she is more profitable than silver and yields better returns than gold. She is more precious than rubies; nothing you desire can compare with her. Long life is in her right hand; in her left hand are riches and honor. Her ways are pleasant ways, and all her paths are peace. She is a tree of life to those who take hold of her; those who hold her fast will be blessed" (Prov. 3:13-18).

In Sophia's last appearance in Proverbs, she invites us to eat the bread and drink the wine she has prepared. How can we heed Lady Wisdom's message and make it a part of our lives? Becoming women of wisdom means following her, opening to the divine in daily life—her ways are insight, life and peace. They are available to us at any age, but become especially important as we move into the second half of life.

As Wisdom celebrates and rejoices in the friendships of women, we honor the God of Mary and Elizabeth, Ruth and Naomi, the God who rejoices in our bonds of friendship. Wisdom walks with us as we care for one another in the sweetness and bitterness of life. Joy is its reward.

PRAYERS TO THE GODDESS

Good morning, Amazing Creator
Goddess so lovely and free
Filled with surprises

What do you have for
Your daughters today?
Marvelous things?

We await your gifts
Each day as the sun
Rises in the sky

Keep us alert and
Expectant, ready
To say thank you

Goddess of the Sea
Wash us clean of the old
Hurts that keep us from
Being new

Rinse away any stains
Of past pains
And repair our souls

Summon us into
Your life-charged water
To bring us new life

We'll give it back

To you
And your other children

Make us to live as
Godmothers to the rest
Of your creations

Caring for, cherishing
Bringing to maturity
All that we know

Make us faithful,
Fulfilled daughters
Worthy of the tasks

At the end of each day
We rest securely in
Your tender arms

One day when our work is done
We will return to the fullness
Of you

When our souls can no longer
Be filled by
Anything else

We will return to you
To be filled
Forever and always

TIME

The old woman watches as the young woman walks on ahead. Near the creek now, she walks over the rocks and broken branches, scattered leaves, once-alive now-dead tree trunks, and roots pulled out by the storms that blow through this canyon.

The cool, clear stream flows very fast in most places, bubbling, splashing. In other places, pools have formed, and the water is still and quiet. The pools are places for the water to rest, it seems.

Life is like that. Of its own accord, it flows, cool and clear, over stones, sand, broken things—but still it flows, and comes to rest in safe, still, quiet pools—places that happen to form or just be there.

This day is such a day, as the old woman watches the young woman walk, almost run up the creek, nimble-of-foot, filled with the excitement that starting a new life brings. She walks upstream, for now the path appears to be easier, less strewn with the red rocks of this canyon, fewer broken limbs and tree roots.

One woman, with fewer years ahead than already lived; one woman with more years ahead than already lived. Each wants the other to know what they know and have not forgotten: the lived wisdom of the old, the vibrant excitement of the young.

The old woman wants to caution the young woman not to walk too much against life's current. It is easier to be carried along with the stream as it flows. This knowledge lies deep within her being, though there have been times during her life that she had to stop, turn around, and follow her inner voice to go against the current. To do so was difficult, even painful, sometimes useless. Other times, she was filled with a new excitement and vision to create a better world. She looks at the young woman, wishing that she might hear the wisdom of the ancestors who live within her and will show her the way. They know when to walk with, and walk against, that life current—they've lived there.

Two women, each belonging to the other. As once the old woman held the young woman's hand to steady her walk, it is now the young woman holding the old woman's hand. Once, "Come, you can do it," came from the old woman's mouth. Now it comes from the young woman's mouth, "Come, Nana, you can do it."

Canyon creek

CHAPTER 5

Sometimes a Stone

LIFE'S CHALLENGES

Let's face it. No one, as the old folks used to say, gets out of this life alive. Or unscathed. I have noticed that the wise and joyful people I have known have managed to see how the difficult times helped them to make sense of life, to find their strength, to learn new things. I know I remember what I've learned from the mistakes I've made or from a disappointment or failed attempt.

During my growing-up years, there were frequent family gatherings. My dad had eleven siblings, my mom had four. I remember one of the family weddings in particular. We always had dancing at these country affairs. I was sitting with my younger cousin. Jack was 11, I think. One of our aunts invited him to the dance floor. She took hold of his hand, knowing if she let go, he'd head for the closest exit! There was a bit, well, maybe a lot of toes stepped on, bumping into other dancers, and cringing expressions, as this dance lesson went on. When the music stopped, Jack came back and another aunt made the suggestion that he had learned something. His quick response, "Yeh, I learned that I'll never do that again!"

Sometimes that is my reaction. Other times, I can find a different way. These challenges have helped to shape who I am today. The memories are healing, some require repairing any damage caused, all have helped me to understand and accept people I meet without judgement since I have no idea what's happening inside them.

4 NOW 1

He left 5 years ago
Passed through the veil
Leaving his disease-ravaged body behind
Freed from this life
Once confined to the earth
Now released

When once there were 4, then 3, then 2, now 1
The other 2 moved away
One has travelled thousands of miles
Across land and sea

One is traveling
In miles not so far
In his life immeasurable distances
To freedom

The 4th one now remains in her home
As her spirit takes flight,
Yet returns
And brings life to her body

The 4th one now the only one, misses the 3
She grieves their absence
Their touch, their voices
Their smiles and frowns

She knows it is the life cycle
That is truth

She reaches into the Divine Energy
Where thinking cannot go

It brings solace
And soothes her soul
And she rests knowing
All is as it is meant to be

A MOTHER'S HEART

A mother's heart stronger than steel
Fragile as a tiny teacup
Don't drop it
Be gentle
Careful

Heartbreak
Pain too great to bear
Hurts deep within her chest
A hurt like no other

Forgive me, so sorry, she cries
Loving too much, her heart
Broken now,
Ever to be made whole again?

She prays it may be so

BECAUSE I LOVE YOU TOO

The wind is screaming
Let me in
It's angry alone afraid
Can't stop
I call as the wind calls
It's cold out here
Let me in

Two lives meet
To share a love
To grow together
Yet apart

Your eyes say you hurt
Your words say it's okay
Your hands say you're reaching
Your body says you're afraid
Your feet say you're running
How do I know?
Because I love you too

COME

My God, I'm tired today
So many people have taken from me
And I had so little to give
But my friend was crying, she needed a hug
My son was confused, he needed to talk
My father was lonely, he needed to share
My husband was burdened, he needed support

I wanted to be alone, to be quiet, to read
To play my guitar
But your people interrupted
And they took what I had to give
I'm tired, drained, weary

Yet now, I know, my God, you
Slipped in with those people, and it was
You who were the giver, and I the taker

SHE LEFT HIM THERE

She stopped in today and left him there
This time the last—she prayed
It was his photo she left
Dropped in the offering box

A ritual expressing her hope for him
For him to find who he is
And love himself
Her faith said he could

She hurt so much
His being ill
Had created a man
She didn't understand
Or even know

So many times she had said
I can't do it anymore
He was in a safe place now
In St. Germaine Church

Oldest church in Paris
It was never finished
As he wasn't
Would he ever be?

She wondered
She prayed
She loved him
She left him there

THE MAN & THE BIRD

That day a tiny bird fell at his feet
Stretched its wings but couldn't fly
He carried it home
In the palm of his hand
And held it there for hours

We must find a place for it, he said
First this call, then another, and another
No one there to help
He would care for it then

He found a dropper
Filled it with water and nourishment
The tiny bird drank, would it live
To fly tomorrow, maybe the next day

All life precious to this man
Unwilling to not save its life
Quiet through the day into the night
The little bird stopped eating, he did too

The morning came, no words spoken
Too painful to say out loud
Dead, during the night its spirit left
The man as silent as the tiny bird

The bird now buried in a safe place
The man filled with sadness
He'll be better
By tomorrow, maybe the next day

THE DAM GAVE OUT

Once again
It happened

The dam gave out
Waters burst forth
Muddy waters
And he was engulfed

As it happens with floods
Others were swept up
In the danger,
The dark, cold, ugly
Current

I'm drowning, she said
He hung onto his raft
And rode it out
What about me,
She cried.

The only answer
The deafening sound
Of angry waters
All around her

Drowning
Once again
And again
And again . . .

She prayed
Great Spirit,
Please rescue me.

CHRISTMAS STORY

As she woke that morning, she heard the carols. They warmed her as she slid slowly out of bed into the cool morning air. And the music reminded her of the special day it was. In her religious beliefs, she knew that Christmas was a day commemorating the Divine becoming human, the perfect taking on the imperfect human form. And because of this, she knew she was connected to God and would someday go home to her Creator.

As she slipped into her robe and slippers, she hummed along to "O Little Town of Bethlehem" and made her way to the kitchen. As the coffee brewed, she glanced around at the tables still cluttered from the Christmas Eve celebration. The eggnog still smelled of the pungent rum and nutmeg. The coffee cups were cold, the gingerbread drying out but still filled with the fragrance of Christmas.

Christmas Eve, their family night—just her husband and their three sons. Each year, what a time they had ooh-ing and ahh-ing over dreamed-of-gifts, giggling at silly ones, and feeling warm in a new sweater.

And this morning the gifts were piled haphazardly near the tree. All had been opened last night, all but the one from her brother. She wanted to save that one for today, for this morning, for when everyone else was still asleep. And now as she poured herself the fresh steaming black coffee into her favorite Christmas mug, she wandered over to the tree. She switched on the tree lights and sat on the sofa, curling her feet under her to preserve the warmth. As she sipped her coffee, she listened to a song about being home for Christmas, then something about a blue Christmas and she wondered why people wrote sad songs for such a happy day. And she daydreamed about the coming day, the friends and family who would come for dinner and the annual exchange of gifts. She hoped everyone would like what she'd made for them.

But now, this brief moment of quiet, she would share with her brother. She picked up his gift, smelled it, squeezed it, and held it close to her heart, pretending this gift of his was much more than the paper and what it held inside. She remembered the many Christmases when they'd been together. She remembered their childhood Christmases on the farm when in early December they would pull an empty sled into the timber down and return with a tree they had chosen and chopped. And their mother would have hot chocolate with marshmallows waiting for them. And the year she was 17. She'd broken up with her boyfriend and she sat late at night crying near the wrapped gifts. He'd come in late too and saw her there and they talked till nearly morning until she was comforted. The warm feelings were tainted by lonely feelings, by the emptiness in her arms. She longed to hug him again. She looked at the tree, saw the little wooden wagon ornament he'd made the Christmas she was 12. He was 14 then, her big, protective brother.

She touched the gift again, then opened it carefully, slowly, lovingly. It was her favorite perfume. She opened it, smelled its familiar scent, dabbed on a tiny, tiny bit, for she knew it must last a very long time. Then she gently replaced the bottle in its box, laid it tenderly back under the tree and walked to the kitchen to begin fixing breakfast. She would think of the perfume often during the day and would remember to put it away that night after all of the Christmas lights were turned off—just as she had done for fourteen years now, since that Christmas he'd first given it to her, and on his way home had hit a patch of black ice. The officer at the front door said, "I'm sorry to tell you . . . "

She would remember, and each Christmas morning, she had resolved, the gift would bring them together again and again.

CHAPTER 6

A Better World

I WANTED TO CHANGE THE WORLD

You see, I have this need to change the world. You'd think I would have figured out by now that I really can't do that. I keep trying though. God knows it. I think God laughs at my delusions of grandeur. I spend time meeting with the important people who make decisions for people like me. They have no right to do that, you know, unless we tell them to. I go downtown and work in the soup kitchen. I am against wars and weapons that destroy. I pray a lot that all people have shelter, food, good work, and feel safe. I probably always will. One thing that I have learned is that I can't do it, but we can.

Bonnie

ONE SON'S STORY

Antonio is the only son of Carmen. Twenty-two years ago, after her husband had been killed by one of the gangs that terrorize the border city of Ciudad Juarez, a pregnant Carmen crossed the border to freedom in El Paso. She had obtained a temorary travel permit, and began to set up her home here in the United States. Antonio was born here, so he is an American Citizen. He grew up with one dream, to help to get legal residency for his mother.

You see, during these last 22 years, Carmen has lived in fear of being deported.

The law didn't permit Antonio to petition for his mother's permanent residency until he reached 21. He entered the Marines at the age of 18 and when he turned 21 this year, the papers he had prepared for so long were finally turned in to the immigration authorities, and the process began to get Carmen her legal residency.

Antonio has just been sent to Iraq. Should he be killed there, we will thank Carmen for the ultimate sacrifice of her son. After she experiences the devastating loss of her son, the process for her residency will stop, for she will have lost the only voice legally recognized on her behalf. If that happens, she will no longer be able to stay in this country that has become her home. As so many others, she will live in fear of deportation to the city where her husband, Antonio's father, was killed so many years ago. "Antonio, please come home safely."

TWO LIVES, ONE STORY

A performance piece

Enter Anne and Maia.

ANNE My name is Anne. I am a woman, a mother. I come from Phoenix. My ex-husband lives in San Diego. My dreams are simple: to have good work and for my children to be happy.

MAIA My name is Maia. I am a woman, a mother. I come from a small village a hundred miles east of Mexico City. My husband died from dysentery last year. My dreams are simple: to have good work and for my children to be happy.

ANNE My family has traveled far and wide in this world. My career has boundless possibilities. One day my company relocated to Mexico City. It meant a big promotion for me. We were moving—how scary—but so exciting!

MAIA My family has stayed close to our tiny village. One day I could no longer feed my family. What would I do? We had to leave our home and go north, how frightening!

ANNE I took my time, packing our belongings, the things we'd need to make the new house our own.

MAIA I had to hurry, my children were starving. We left all behind, taking only what fit into our backpacks and the money needed to pay the coyotes to get us across the border—and some tortillas.

ANNE It would be a wonderful adventure moving across the land. We would fly, the children and I, while a moving van carried our things.

MAIA It would be a treacherous trip across the land, so we'd been told. We had no choice. There was work there—work that no one else wanted to do. We had to go.

ANNE Our family and friends gathered around us to say goodbye. We would miss each other very much.

MAIA Our village came together to pray for us as we left with six others. My mother and sister hugged us goodbye. We held each other a very long time, wondering, would we ever be together again? "Vaya con Dios, Maia"—Go with God, my dear Maia—my mother had said.

ANNE The trip went well. I could look out the window and see the vast desert below. The pilot said it was 110. Thank God, we were high above that heat. The onboard movie helped to keep the children from being bored, and the meal was pretty good.

MAIA We could not have imagined the dangers, the miles and miles of sand, scrub brush, and cactus, the hunger, the thirst, the sun, how it burned. The nights were filled with strange sounds, fear and darkness. Such darkness.

ANNE Our plane easily navigated from the U.S. to Mexico. Borders, after all, are just lines on paper, aren't they?

MAIA The coyotes took $2,000 for me and $600 for the children, money we'd borrowed from our family and friends and would pay back as soon as I started to work. They promised us safe passage across the border.

ANNE My daughter got sick from the excitement. She always does. The flight attendant brought water and medicine, and she was fine.

MAIA My son couldn't go on. There was no water. We buried him under a tree, where the shade would keep him cool.

ANNE The children and I moved into our new neighborhood surrounded by other families like ours. We unpacked and settled in, me in my new job, the children in their school. This would be home for awhile.

MAIA We finally reached the city and moved in with my cousin, crowded yes, with his wife and three children. I was so afraid and I cried for my dead son. I began work cleaning houses, my two little girls went to school. I wondered, could we become citizens of this new country?

ANNE There were times when the people on the street weren't friendly, but the people in our neighborhood offered us their friendship. The authorities loved us.

MAIA Then something happened. Where we had been tolerated before, we were now suspect. Some people in the government said we shouldn't go to the doctor when we were sick, the kids shouldn't be allowed in the schools. I desperately wanted to fit in, and was learning English so we could. The authorities hated us.

ANNE We traveled around the city, finding art galleries, good restaurants, and special stores, enjoying the newness of it all. I was becoming successful, my children happy. Strangers in a strange land . . . We thrived.

MAIA We lived in fear, what if immigration discovered us? Strangers in a strange land. I wanted us to become part of this wonderful country that held so much potential. I even started a better job in a restaurant. I wanted for my children to have the chance to be healthy and to learn so they could get good jobs.

Pause.

MAIA I cannot go home. I cannot become a citizen. I live in limbo. My dreams remain simple: to have good work and for my children to be happy.

ANNE My work in Mexico is finished, and we have returned home. My dreams remain simple: to have good work and for my children to be happy.

MAIA I met a woman last night. She had a nice smile and gentle eyes. She said her name was Anne—a mother just like me, I think.

ANNE We went out to dinner last night. I felt homesick for Mexico when I came face to face with a small woman clearing a table. Her name tag said Maia. I wonder, is she a mother just like me?

All exit.

A PEOPLE OF HEART & SOUL

I met two people last night on a movie screen in a downtown Scottsdale theater. This film, *El Norte*, tells the story of a brother and sister, undocumented immigrants from Guatemala. Their story is archetypal of thousands of refugees who flee injustices, hunger, and danger to the North in search of a better life.

This is a story of death, murder and injustice. We see the parents being killed, the sister dying of typhus caused by bites of hundreds of crazed, squealing rats as she crawled through a rancid sewer to reach the North. And it is the death of a young man's dream to fulfill his father's wish to be accepted and be known not as undocumented cheap labor, but as "a man of heart and soul."

It is not a hopeful story, as much as romanticists like me would like it to be. But it is truth. Many fear what they call "a horde from the South" that they insist will undermine our economy. They say we must turn back their experience, their rich culture, their beauty and their wisdom. Must we?

We are a country of immigrants. The first sight of the United States for many people was the Statue of Liberty. Standing in the New York Harbor, it is engraved with the words of Emma Lazarus, "Give me your tired, your poor, your huddled masses yearning to breathe free, the wretched refuse of your teeming shore. Send these, the homeless, the tempest-tost to me, I lift my lamp beside the golden door." We believed that once. Do we still?

DREAM DREAMS

We are never alone.
When we gather with others in all the Holy Names of God, seeking wisdom, understanding and guidance, we reconnect, we share, we reaffirm our connection with one another and with the Supreme Creator of all. We come with openness that we may see more clearly. We come as searchers and dreamers.

We dream dreams. Dreams come and go in our lives. If one dream dies, another can be born.

We have our own dreams just for us. The dreams we had as children, as 20-, 30-, 40-year-olds probably were different than today's dreams. Today they are more flexible than yesterday. Our dreams plow the rough ground to make them real.

So too with our world; our world yearns for a new dream.

We dream together of the world Jesus talked about. When we join together, we can say yes to the challenge to make that dream come true.

Nothing is beyond our reach if we reach out together, if we reach out with confidence based on our values and knowledge. If we are willing to persevere even in difficult times, such as these. If we rejoice with every small step forward. If we dream those dreams that will transform our lives, our world.

Nothing is impossible if we put aside our fears. If we build our dreams with faith and hope—in ourselves, in our sisters and brothers, and, above everything, in the Maker of All.

We dream a world where all people have shelter, food, freedom to be all they were created to be. We see it today in the boy who makes and sells cupcakes to benefit people who are hungry, the workers who care for those who are sick, the homeowner who leaves treats at the front door for those who deliver packages, strangers giving water and food to a hungry man, a hat to a woman on a corner. We see it in citizens' petitions to provide decent living spaces for prisoners, housing for the mentally ill, a hand up for those with substance abuse issues. We dream a world where all life is honored, all creatures, the earth itself.

Without a dream, there is only death. A dream says yes to life.

AN ORDINARY SUNDAY

Here is what happened to me one Sunday morning. It was a couple of weeks since my son had left the United States for the United Kingdom. He was beginning the next lap of his life journey with a teaching position at the University of Portsmouth. Portsmouth captivated his interest and imagination and with a job offer, he couldn't resist the call.

I was missing him terribly already and feeling sad and lonely. My destination that morning was my prayer place, followed by sharing food with my friends. Nearly halfway there, the tears began to flow, washing my face as I drove. Unable to see clearly, I turned into a parking lot and passed a man sitting on the corner with the familiar sign, "Will work for food." Today, the signs read, "Help, homeless, hungry, can't feed my family." Many variations, all being held in hands not recently washed and faces filled with desperation.

I sat in my car for a bit, aware that my prayer that day would not be with my friends. The food I was to share was simple—bread and cheese. It would help the man on the corner, I thought. I returned the way I came and he walked over when I opened my window. As we looked at each other, I told him that I didn't have any money but would he like the bread and cheese. He took the food and thanked me. Then he looked directly into my eyes and asked, "Are YOU okay?" I knew if I spoke, it would be through tears, so I just nodded.

Feeling humble and grateful for his recognizing my sadness, I began to drive away. I glanced back, and as people who are homeless do, he had disappeared.

Deep within, I heard, "Give as much as you can, it will be returned to you a hundredfold."

THE END

The door slammed
He was gone
She alone remained
It was over, done

Their marriage
Once filled with so much love
That love had turned to disgust
Then nothing

Alcohol his new mistress
One drink was too many
And one was never enough
Until he fell into bed

Once she waited for him
With excitement and yearning
Then fear and dread
Relieved when he just passed out

As grains of sand trickle
Through an open hand
Their love for one another
Slowly slipped away
Not one grain remained

Only she had courage
To say enough, to end it
He must leave
The home they'd created together

So many years together, now alone
And life continued seemingly as it was
The sound of the door closing violently
Echoed in the now empty room

He walked away
Confronted with only himself
Alone
Both alone

The hurt and hollowness
Nearly consuming them
Yet, no one will see the broken hearts
That keep beating as before

He'll go to work in the morning
The pain so deep in his heart
Like a knife had plunged into his chest
No one can know

She'll go to work in the morning
As if nothing has changed
She can't show on the outside
What is destroying her inside

How many days will it go on?
She doesn't know
Her faith tells her someday
She will be okay again
He might too

BUT I'M JUST A KID

Orphan: A child left without parents? A person with schizophrenia who has trouble keeping friends? A man who has lost his job, then steals food and ends up in jail? A woman who didn't think addiction could happen to her? All orphans. All alone and lonely.

Let me tell you about an orphan I know.

Matt is 16. His mother committed suicide last summer. His dad doesn't want him. He lives with his grandma.

I sat down with him one day and just said, "How are you, really?"

To my surprise, he told me. "I'm not worth very much. I think I'm an orphan. Grandma tries, but she doesn't get it. I have friends she doesn't like. I'm not one of the cool kids. I have trouble with a lot of stuff.

I really loved my mom, and then she goes and offs herself. Gary, that's my dad, he called two days later, told me he was sorry, said he'd stay in touch. He didn't, he lied again.

I just go to school everyday, except when I skip, then I get in trouble. The counselor says I get one more chance, then I get another and another. So far, just counseling. Then I either hang out with my friends or come home and go on the internet or play my music—really loud. Grandma hates that.

Yeah, I've done a lot—run away whenever I feel like it. Hang out with a crowd that the counselor says if I keep it up I'll have to leave Grandma's house and go to detention. From what I've heard I don't want to do that.

They say I keep testing my limits. Well, maybe that's how they see it. I'm mixed up. The only time I'm happy is when I smoke my pot or when I mix cold medicines, you know, stuff like that. Then I'm happy—I don't remember that my mom killed herself, that I have a dad who doesn't give a darn about me. But then I'm not worth anything, anyway, so why would he?

Grandma says she cares, I guess she does, she yells a lot, says she doesn't get it, calls my aunts. She's tired, I guess. She's poor too.

Sometimes my cousins come. We have a lot of fun together, especially the girl ones. They love to dance and pull me along with them till I feel the music. Then I'm happy too. Till I remember.

I'm alone and I'm scared but I can't tell anyone that. My mom used to call me her little man. How many kids my age you know who've been to the mental ward a dozen times or more visiting their mom? And then two weeks ago I was there—got too high on the cold medicines I mixed, I guess. Grandma called the rescue squad, and there I was.

I don't want to be like my mom was.

They tell me they love me, that I am lovable. They tell me I'm good, that I can do big things. I want to believe that. They tell me I can use what is happening to me to help other people someday. Not yet, but someday. They tell me there is a God who loves me even when I think I'm not worth anything. I don't know if I believe any of that, but keep telling me, please. It's all I have."

THE GIFT OF LIFE

*A performance piece, written for The Donor Network,
inspired by stories that parents told me of their loved
ones who had requested, when they died to this life, that
their organs to be donated to save the life of another*

∞

*Enter parents.
One, parent of son.
Two, parent of daughter.*

ONE The test was positive. We would be parents in
September. I dreamed of the day when my baby would
be born.

TWO We had tried for so long. The day had come. We
were pregnant. I dreamed of my baby's birth.

ONE When I saw my son for the first time, I marveled
at the miracle he was. His fingers were perfect, and
I quickly checked his toes to see if they were okay.
Because if toes are okay, that means everything is.
They were. And I dreamed of bringing him home to the
Winnie-the-Pooh nursery that we'd prepared for him.

TWO When I saw my daughter for the first time, I
looked with amazement at the wonder I saw in her
eyes, her big, beautiful, blue eyes. Surely, those eyes
were the mirror to an exquisite soul. And I dreamed

of seeing her in the room decorated with bunnies that we'd just finished.

ONE As my son grew, I loved him, fussed at him, taught and learned from him. I watched my fearless child go off to school into a world that was his own. And he grew tall, my son, into a handsome little boy, then adolescent and young man. I dreamed of sending him off to college.

TWO My daughter, oh, what a charmer, she drew everyone to her. Who could resist this young woman, so full of life? Certainly the boys couldn't! As we drove to her high school graduation, I dreamed of the future that would be hers.

ONE Into the work world he went. Job hunting was so hard. He got good at interviewing. God knows, he had enough of them! Eventually, I think someone felt sorry for him and said, come work for me. Ah, he was on the way. I dreamed he would find his path.

TWO Fresh out of college and filled with enthusiasm and hope in what might be, she was off into the big, wide world. I don't know if it was her talent or her beauty. Maybe it was her cooking, her specialty chocolate chip cookies. Something worked. She was hired immediately and called excitedly, Mom, Dad, I got the job! Oh, but we weren't surprised. I dreamed big things for her.

ONE His whole life lay before him.

TWO Her whole life lay before her.

ONE The phone was ringing. Who could it be? The hospital? What? My son had a what? It wasn't possible, he was too young for a heart attack. The only thing that would save this young man's life, they said, was a new heart. We waited and waited and waited. After five months, time was running out. I prayed for a heart to become available. Stop, what was I doing? To find one, another must die. I didn't want that. I continued to pray. What else could I do? I had nightmares of losing my son.

TWO Someone was at the door. My daughter's friend, Jeremy. There was an accident? But where was she? How was she? What? Hospital. No, it could not be. I stared into her beautiful eyes, as big and blue as always. But now they stared blankly at the ceiling. I dreamed of hearing her voice again.

ONE He couldn't last much longer. He told us that if he didn't make it, he wanted to donate his healthy organs to someone else. These months had taught us how very precious life is, and he said he couldn't withhold healing and life to someone else if a heart couldn't be found for him. We loved each other as much as we could and dreamed that tomorrow he would still be here.

TWO We held out a faint hope she'd come back. But there was too much damage. We remembered that if anything should happen, she wanted to donate her organs. Once more I looked into her beautiful eyes and asked her, knowing she couldn't hear me. Once more I told her how very much I loved her. I dreamed of her resting in the Creator's loving arms. And I dreamed of life without her.

ONE He was home. He had been given new life through the generosity of a stranger. It would be a long time, but he would one day love and work and play as he had before. But, with, oh, so much more appreciation of the value of life. With hope, we dreamed again.

TWO I didn't want to get out of bed. My friends told me I should be done grieving, but I wasn't. She wasn't even able to say goodbye. No last hug. I missed her. I knew somehow my grief was a pure sign of the love I had for her and I knew that she lived on, not only through those who received her organs but in the love I felt for her everyday. She would be forever in my heart and I would remember her. I dreamed of a day when I wouldn't feel so sad.

ONE My son had returned to work. He'd written a letter to the family who gave him their daughter's heart. He didn't know what to say. He said he thanked them and he would live his life remembering her. We dreamed of tomorrow.

TWO It had been a year. Still I ached for my daughter. I knew she was still here—just like the wind, I couldn't see her, but I could feel her. Sometimes it was like a gentle breeze caressing my cheek, sometimes it was like a gust that cooled my warm body. I dreamed of her in the wee hours of the morning.

ONE Each day I prayed for the young woman who gave my son new life. She lived on in him, and as I watched him in his quiet moments, I knew that he was grateful. While her soul rested peacefully, her heart beat rhythmically in the chest of my son as he went on his daily run. I was dreaming new dreams.

TWO I found the letter the other day—the one we got from the young man who had her heart. I had put it away all these months, unopened. It was time to read it. I hoped it would give me the ironic chance to cherish and reaffirm life. I hoped it would lessen the pain in the pit of my own wrenching grief and turmoil of my daughter's death. I was gently reminded that the option to donate was its own gift. I began to dream new dreams.

ONE He'd gone and got himself engaged. He was into body building, he cooked, he baked. He baked chocolate chip cookies—a lot! He was alive. Life, a precious treasure to be reminded of each second of each day. I dreamed of a daughter-in-law and grandchildren.

TWO I know she lives on in him and in all of the other people who received her organs. That would make her happy. It consoles me. I believe a day will come when it won't hurt so much and I can smile when I see other blue eyes. I dream that day will come—someday.

ONE I often wonder how the mom of the young woman is doing. I would like to meet her, but then again, what would I say? I'm sorry? I wish things could have been different for you? I'm sad for you? I pray for you? There are no words that seem adequate. Maybe I could just hold her and let my arms tell her what words cannot say.

All exit.

DESERT PILGRIM

Written by James G. Danowski, inspired by Isaiah 45:23

Pilgrim, did you hear the quiet?
Pilgrim, did you see the empty?
    Do you walk, traveling on to nowhere?
    Do you wonder, is there someone out there?

Desert Pilgrim, did the sun rise?
    Has the wind blown?
    Did the bird sing?

Desert, I didn't want your water
Mountain, take away your valley
Fire, I can't find your cool breeze
Snowfall, I don't see your warm leaves

Desert Pilgrim, is the moon full?
    Have the clouds come?
    Did the rain fall?

Children, in the silence I hear you!
Nameless, in the dark I find you!
    Alone and confused, there I will find you!
    My sun rises, my birds sing just for you!

Desert Pilgrim, I am with you
    All of your days
    All of your nights

Patience, sounds will soon delight you
Injury, colors soon will bathe you
  You'll be dancing, with the hopes of ages
  Singing with me, filling the dreams of each one

Desert Pilgrim, will you hold me?
  Will you tell me?
  Will we laugh?

ONCE MORE THE DESERT

Nevada Nuclear Weapons Test Site

Once more the desert
Lost amidst the sand and rocks and sagebrush
Is buried devastation
Melted earth core
Heated, expanded, contracted
Damaged, destroyed, desacralized

Once more the desert
A journey now complete
Begun 7 years ago on a cold weekend in January
And finished now on a balmy March day

Completed, searching pilgrimage
To understand the violence of this nuclear madness
And finding also the violence within ourselves

Once more the desert
To know what is nonviolent
We must know what is violent
And allow it to be chiseled, dug and ripped
From within and around us

Then, only then, can we come face to face
With the experience of truth
Within ourselves, our God,
And you, my brothers and sisters,

Once more the desert
This time
Farewell

Let there be peace
In all people and all places

∞

A Prayer for the End of Nuclear Weapons Testing

God of faithfulness and promise,
Lover of all creation,
Hear our prayer for an end to
Nuclear weapons testing.

You named us prophets to preserve
And nurture your creation:
All peoples, all life.
Indeed, the earth itself.

Enlighten our efforts to end
Nuclear weapons testing;
Energize our wills for the
Restoration of creation.

Inspire and guide all who pray
And work nonviolently,
So that your promised peace will
Fill our world with lives
Rich in your love.
Amen

∞

The above prayer was written while Bonnie Danowski served as a Nevada Desert Experience Board Member in December, 1990. It was printed on a card and circulated within the communities dedicated to nonviolence and non-nuclear proliferation. In 1996, the U.N. General Assembly developed The Comprehensive Test Ban Treaty. It has been signed by 183 countries, ratified by 166. The United States has stopped testing.

III

FOG, LIGHT, SUN & MOON

He has gone, yet I feel his presence.
He is near, how can that be? His spirit left—
came, left, came, left—his body so worn and
wounded, a prison for such a free holy spirit,
who is now dancing among the stars.

CHAPTER 7

The Last Goodbye

HE CAME, HE STAYED, HE LEFT

One September night this man walked into my life, this man who would become my husband. He stayed a long time and left as quickly as he'd come.

This is how it all began. We were both pretty new to Phoenix. St. Mary's Church, in the heart of the city, attracted Jim after he'd stopped in Phoenix on his way to settle in Los Angeles. I too found this church staffed by Franciscan friars when I got here on my way to Tucson. Jim from Wisconsin, me from Iowa, he was fresh out of the U.S. Air Force, I from Iowa State University.

Needless to say, he didn't get to Los Angeles, I didn't make it to Tucson.

This city has been built on people from everywhere, adventurous folks, independent and self-assured, looking for a new start. Because of that, the friars at St. Mary's provided a space for young singles to meet and form a support system, often resulting in lifelong friendships—and even marriages.

So it was that Jim and I were new to the area, and we were invited to a party. Little did either of us know what would happen after that. My first big outing, I was filled with nervousness, yet when I rang the doorbell, I was welcomed with hugs, introductions, and genuine caring.

Soon after, this guy came through the door—sideburns, plaid flannel shirt, deck shoes with the toes cut out. Who is this guy, not a great sense of style, I must say. He was interesting though. His strange dress was explained later when I found out he was working for the Cursillo Movement, a Catholic weekend experience. His pay: room and board and $40 each month to spend as he chose. You can guess I didn't marry him for his money!

From that first meeting in September of 1963, we didn't miss a day without talking with or seeing each other. No dates, nothing romantic at all, but a friendship, a partnership you might say, formed that became the solid foundation of our lives.

Eleven months later we were married.

Those first years were filled with getting to know each other and our dreams of the years to come. Our paths converged and the smooth path became riddled with stones and twists and turns.

At the age of 31, Jim was diagnosed with Multiple Sclerosis. Life had been getting harder before his diagnosis, especially when no one could say what was happening. He'd miss work, his vision would double, he limped, his brain was fuzzy, he was in pain and tired all of the time. So, having the diagnosis was better than not knowing, but it certainly wasn't what we were expecting or hoping for.

Forty-two years after his diagnosis, on a sunny Arizona day in September, my soulmate, my husband, Jim, took his last breath, died to this life. His spirit flew, free again.

We cried, we smiled, we waved goodbye with the promise we would meet again.

"YES"

"So you will be my people, and I will be your God," (Jer. 30:22). Jim and I believed this promise, that God would walk with us all the days of our lives. We knew we would never be alone. We looked at each other at our engagement and naively said, *"YES."*

Our wedding day came. We knew each other a little better, knew some of our dreams, our hopes, joys, fears. We believed that our God would always be with us. We looked at each other under a beautiful Arizona sun and said, *"YES."*

My first pregnancy, a miscarriage. Though it was a huge loss, we couldn't share our feelings with each other very well. In our confusion, our hurt and our loss, we said a trembling *"YES."*

Our Mike was born, all of 4 pounds—such a tiny, teeny life, our son. The doctors said he was a miracle. Of course, he was. We were thrilled, he was beautiful, our baby. We looked at each other in disbelief and said, *"YES."*

A few weeks later, we left our beloved desert and returned to the verdant pastures of the Midwest to be near family. A year or so later, Chris was born. A healthy, laughing, happy infant, who soon began singing songs in his crib. Now we were four. Did we have enough love to give to this newest member of our family? We looked at each other in wonder and said, *"YES."*

Illness came—an unwelcome intruder that moved into our family. No one knew what it was. All we knew was that Jim was sick. Without income, our house was gone, the little Volkswagen he'd given me for my birthday was sold. I went back to work, friends watched our boys, Jim spent ten weeks in the hospital. Finally a diagnosis: Multiple Sclerosis. He won't get well. *No.* He won't work again. *No.* The disease will progress. *No.* He may lose his sight, use of his legs, arms, hands. *No.* He may live in pain the rest of his life. *No, no, no, no.* Where are you, God? "If you will be my people, I will be your God." What? How can this be? We didn't know why, but we still believed. Our hearts breaking, we whispered a quivering, reluctant, *"YES."*

We picked up what we had left of our lives and returned to the Arizona desert where we had met those several years before—with new dreams, and the task of rebuilding our lives began. Jim might be in pain, they said, but we still had much of our lives to live. The brokenness was mending, our boys grew from tots to children to teenagers to adults. There were hills to climb, mountains at times, and valleys too deep, rivers too wide, to navigate on our own. Still, our faith was strong—most of the time. "If you will be my people, I will be your God." Again, we said, *"YES."*

We managed through those times only because we believed that we would be okay, that the challenges facing our family could be overcome and make us stronger. Some of the times we weathered tornadoes, other times calm, sunny skies. We survived each crisis. We knew we could make a difference in our world—as long as we were together, more confidently now, the answer was *"YES."*

Middle age brought security, understanding, and much joy. We were able to dedicate our lives to helping others through programs we developed in communication, and enrichment for engaged and married couples. Jim's artistic bent came out in many paintings, watercolors, oils, pastels. His guitar was taken from the closet, and we had family sing-alongs. I went back to school, then found a career with the Franciscans in justice and peace work. Spending time together, always sharing our spirituality with one another, it was easier to say "*YES.*"

This time of life also brought more Multiple Sclerosis symptoms, more physical, emotional and mental pain, more difficulties for Jim. For me, life brought its own challenges with my concern for him. The strain of living with his MS and the heavy lifting that I had to do because he couldn't were catching up with me. These new hurdles led to the now-familiar "*YES.*"

Then it happened—the beginning of our parting. Cancer, cancer treatment, a fall and broken shoulder surgery, cancer again, left untreated, a return to surgery. After surgery, we found out the cancer was racing through his body. Life changed that day. We'd fought battles, the war waged on, and this time we knew it was bigger than us. Our love for one another deepened to a level never reached before. We continued to say, "*YES.*"

Jim left his broken, tired body on September 4, 2013. His spirit, the true essence of who he was remains, I'm positive. I used to ask "why" a lot. No more. Now I know for certain, "If you will be my people, I will be your God, and I will walk with you all the days of your lives." I still say "*YES.*"

As I read this today, more than eight years later, I miss my best friend, confidant, husband, partner, muse. I rejoice that he is no longer hurting and is safe. I am too. Every moment of every day I am filled with gratitude. "*YES.*" May it always be so.

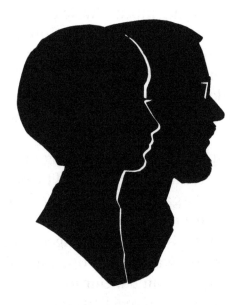

Bonnie & Jim (die-cut)

ABOVE THE CLOUDS SOMEWHERE

Above the clouds somewhere between Charlotte and Phoenix, I remember a time when Jim and I were traveling home from a conference. Seems so many years ago.

We had developed a marriage enrichment program that was going well. However, it didn't fit the criteria of a larger, much more powerful organization. By the end of the conference, we resigned ourselves to let go of what we had been doing.

We'd been through losses before. We knew what we'd had was good for the people who had experienced it. We would file it away now and wait for the Spirit to knock with something new. Still, we were sad and felt betrayed. We'd recovered before. Death of one dream always led to a new dream. Multiple Sclerosis took one dream, we dreamed another.

Our hearts forever united, we were to make new dreams again, some we would share, others we wouldn't. One time we were talking about the future. I asked Jim what were his dreams. He said, "That's almost an unfair question. I hope to get through the day."

That's when I knew I had choices to make. There was no cure for his disease, but my life had to be more—I had to build a future.

It might or might not include Jim. I had much more to do. He would always be my love, my home, my foundation, my touchstone, and my muse.

"Build it well, it must sustain you when I am gone," he said without saying it. He believed that, I did too. We, he, I would be ok. And all would be well.

He is gone now. I remember that moment after the conference Jim and I had attended, when we were flying home at 36,000 feet. My prayer: "God of All, Mysterious Presence, 36,000 feet above the earth, I can see forever. Am I in there somewhere? I hope so."

THE LAST GOODBYE

July 25, 2013

I was paralyzed this morning with this whole cancer thing. I'm feeling really scared and sad. It's weird, but I'm reacting as if Jim is already very close to dying, even though intellectually I know he isn't.

Shock, denial, fear of the unknown of tomorrow of the future.

He's having more pain and I called Jim's doctor to tell her he wants a longer-acting pain med. I think that is morphine. That scares me too.

What on earth will I do? I'm feeling so responsible for everything and inadequate to be the responsible one. I wish my son Chris were home—2 ½ more weeks.

My energy is depleted, and I'm isolating. Don't want to talk about this and when I do, I cry. I'm frustrated and angry that the hospital isn't calling back, and it seems like the doctors won't do anything for Jim. We just wait and wait. And I can't seem to be able to do anything about it. I don't know if I should call the surgeon or not.

Jim wants chemo if offered, which disqualifies him from hospice. He's okay with that because he can keep his nursing assistant. She's awfully good at what she does and maybe we should just pay her.

The emptiness I'm feeling is almost overwhelming. I haven't found a way to feel better. I'm just sad, so sad.

August 4

I guess we have entered the new and final chapter of our life together. My Jim is going away—fading from the man I've known for so long, the man I've given my everything to. He's in the last months of this life. I fear he won't go gently, but with pain and medications that all have side effects that change who he is. But, not really. They just change the outside part. His spirit will always be the good, kind and generous man I've known. I am so sad today—for him, for us.

Eternal Living Presence, be my courage, bring forth unselfishness and love so I can do this. May I be grateful and graceful during this last part of our journey. May I be a good person. May I take good care of him. Give me energy, courage, strength, and love.

May I be the channel of your love. Give me what is needed to be your instrument. Keep me strong. Teach me your ways, Jesus, my Brother, help me to do what you would do and how you would do it. Teach me your ways. Show me how to be love.

Once we bought a tiny statue, an old woman and old man sitting on a park bench. That's who we'd be one day. We were young then, filled with dreams. We would walk into old age, hand in hand. Not to be, not to be.

August 12

Oncologist appointment this morning. The doctor keeps saying stats are only stats and won't say anything about Jim's life expectancy. He knows how the pain has suddenly increased but won't say anything else. Another appointment in 4 weeks, unless there are changes.

I feel so confused, so unclear—how can they suggest hospice, when there was a PET scan showing no cancer? I just feel helpless in all of this. I feel unattractive, old, and inadequate to handle anything. My arm hurts. I'm having ocular migraines, and I am anxious about everything, My chest feels empty. I'm afraid. I am a mess.

Where is my God? My rescuer? Jesus, why are you so far away? Who do I turn to? This pain is consuming me.

This isn't all about me. How selfish can I be? How can I help Jim? He is the one who needs support. If not me, who?

Jesus, teach me to be unselfish, to live my life out of love as you did. It doesn't matter what anyone else thinks or says. It matters how Jim is . . . Help . . .

I sense I must go to the charnal ground, the place of dying and death.

I think I just did.

August 19

This morning my daily centering time was interrupted by tears—again—who do I cry for? Jim? I hear him moan. He says it hurts when he moves. So whether asleep or awake I hear sounds of his pain.

It makes me cry. I can't help it. It hurts so much, and I can do so little.

Do I cry for him? Do I cry for me? Crying for me feels so selfish. I don't want to cry for me, I don't. Again, I am helpless, it seems.

I cry for us. In 3 days we'll be married 49 years—our last anniversary if all indicators are right. Tears fall. I try to hold them back—failing, even at that. I can't do much right these days.

We had "Three for Eternity" engraved on our wedding bands—Jim, me, and God. Our God is here or I'd totally fall apart, I'm sure. Yet, I am so, so sad. I cry for the boys. They both need their dad. He's slipping so fast. I fear my inner drama queen coming out. I don't know what I'm supposed to feel—I don't think it is this. Or if it is, I want this need for attention to take me to a new place where I feel empowered to be strong and unselfish.

Stop feeling sorry for myself. Start living. Live each moment in the present. Stop living in the future—it may not come, certainly not the way I think.

Universal Mystery, God, the One Who Is All That Is, may I get in touch with You so I can do what I need to do. I need Your wisdom, strength, guidance, judgment.

My sons, Mike and Chris, need to be consoled. They need a mother who is strong and wise. I want to be her.

August 20

7:20 a.m., and I'm feeling better today. After being told by the hospice counselors that my grieving is normal. Knowing that, I guess I feel better. Both of them thought it was a good idea to take 2 nights away so that I could cry whenever I needed to, and to follow my own advice from the caregiving classes I've taught. It's hard though—it feels like Jim doesn't want me to leave him for even an hour. He and I have to be talking more. I'm feeling really alienated and alone in this and embarrassed that I'm such a mess.

Today I have physical therapy, lunch with friends and happy hour later with other friends. Sounds like a day just for me. Why do I need more? That should be enough, shouldn't it?

Our hospice social worker said in her six years as a social worker, she has never seen anyone cured. The mixed messages from hospice and the oncologist are driving me crazy.

Acceptance versus giving up is a concept I must explore. Acceptance will allow me to live in the present, enjoy today, do what I can. Giving up is just quitting on everything. No appreciation of today.

I have to get my body under control—arms, whole back, hips, legs. I'm having so much pain through those areas.

August 22—Morning

It's 4:30 a.m. He sleeps beside me, as he has these 49 years. I am complete in this marriage, in this life he and I chose so long ago. The many births and deaths, wins and losses—gifts all, though not always recognized as gifts at the time. We are who we are, this life, this journey, this blessing. We won't see our 50th anniversary unless there's a miracle. The grand finale will come. Will he—will I—will we be ready?

August 22—Evening

The medical world is made up of people like every other profession. Different physicians have different views. We are at a point where we're getting conflicting opinions from different hospitals, and we're unsure of what to do next.

Jim's lab work indicates the cancer is growing and his body is unable to stop it; the doctors are disagreeing whether chemotherapy would help. Jim is a 100% disabled service-connected veteran, the class of veterans who receive the best care allowed—but what if we want to pursue treatment outside of what his insurance approves? I say we'll pay for it.

While meeting with the surgeons, one of them takes Jim out of the room, the other has a heart to heart with me. They are concerned that without chemotherapy, Jim will not live much longer. It is Jim's and my decision.

On our way home, I looked at my husband and told him what the surgeon had said. We are accustomed to making decisions together. Chemotherapy or no chemotherapy, though, was Jim's to make. It would lengthen his life, but chemo has side effects. Whether I agreed or not, I promised to support him no matter what his decision. I meant it.

Jim said he does NOT want chemo.

It is our 49th anniversary. Jim is dying of cancer. We won't have a 50th anniversary without a miracle.

I write often, but now I want to be even more faithful to this journal, so that I remember, so that our sons remember, so that we don't lose these months.

Caring for Jim has become a 24/7 role I play now, and I get tired and cranky sometimes. I overreact, Jim underreacts. I get frustrated sometimes when he doesn't want to take his pain meds.

Our life together continues as it began—two people loving each other, walking hand in hand, and grateful for every moment. A last chapter and an end—a chapter and end that I don't want to write, don't want to live— but I do want to remember.

It will be challenging but ok, as it has been these 49 years. In the end, all shall be well, and I will celebrate Jim's life, our life, our gift to this world and all that is in it. We have been given the gift of life, and it is our privilege and destiny to do nothing less than give it back. As night closes in, I look forward to the closeness of sleep and rest and peace.

August 25

I've heard it said that acceptance brings peace, a new way, a good way to live, I think. I'm of German-Irish descent, we can be a wee bit headstrong. I've had my struggles. Those struggles have melted away the icy shell of who I really am. Within that core is trust and belief. The Universal Mystery lives there. I've found a new peace, a new kind of love, and a new way to live. There is no question—all will be well.

September 1

Sunday again, and we are quiet today. Jim sleeps off and on throughout the day. Pain fills our home. His body is filled with the pain of the cancer growing within him. His heart is filled with the pain that sadness brings. He remains quiet but for the times he moans in his sleep when it hurts too much. Deep within I know he is suffering today in all ways. My heart breaking, I can only watch, soothe him with touches and soft words and keep pain meds on schedule.

Sunday nights are always special family dinners. One of his favorites tonight, pizza, and he joins the rest of us, a bit more quiet but present to everyone. Our granddaughter, Elli, her mom, my former daughter-in-law, Tam, and her new husband, Gerry, leave a little earlier than usual.

We, too, go to bed a little earlier, and we both fall asleep soon after our usual, "Good night, I love you. God bless you. See you in the morning."

∞

September 2—Monday, Labor Day

3 A.M. Jim sits up, screams, filled with fear. "Call somebody, Bon, call somebody. Hurry." (Bon was Jim's love name for me.)

I immediately call hospice and they tell me to give him a Haldol and a quick-release oxycodone. The nurse is on her way. He begins to calm down as I hold him and tell him it's okay. He is jerking and so afraid. What is happening?

I just know I must calm him, wait for the nurse, pray his fear goes away. What is he afraid of? He won't say. He is very scared.

Thank God, the nurse gets to the house quickly to check on him, I'm not sure whether she is giving him more medications. He does go back to sleep. She stays till 5:30 a.m., and we sit at the kitchen table as she does her notes. I think she's doing her notes at our house because she doesn't feel safe to leave. But Jim remains stable, resting—knocked out, actually—so she leaves. I am so grateful she was here.

I go back to bed, put my arm around Jim, hold my head close to his chest. He doesn't notice, and I fall back to sleep.

7 *A.M.* He wakes again, jerking, afraid, "get up, get up." He wants to go to his recliner, I try to help him into his wheelchair, but I'm not holding tightly enough and he slips to the floor. Somehow we manage to get him into his wheelchair, and I push him into the family room to his recliner.

Jim can't get comfortable, wants a coke, then pillows under, all around him. He wants his feet up, down, up, down. More coke.

I call Chris, and he and his girlfriend, Heather, come right away. I can't reach Mike, who is away on a camping trip. Soon, Jim is down to two words used intermittently, feet, coke, feet, coke, feet, coke. Nothing soothes him. I am afraid to call hospice, but Chris says I must. It is time.

The nurse comes quickly, a different one, new to this job, she says. I can't remember, did she give him more meds? His restlessness continues, and at 7:30 a.m. we all decide that he must go to a hospice center—to get his meds adjusted, so we think.

He had fought leaving the house the past 2 months or so. He had said no, home was where he was comfortable. He had refused to go to the hospital—not even to get his meds adjusted, when he had thought they weren't working for him.

We wait as the nurse looks for a bed somewhere. She finds one after searching, commenting she is new and doesn't know the ropes yet. Finally, she finds a bed. He will go to the hospice center.

I'm sorry, so sorry, Jim. I know you didn't want to leave our home. I wonder, could we have kept you home? This plagues me still. Please forgive me for that decision. No one in the house that morning felt you could stay home. You were so afraid and so uncomfortable. But why didn't I insist they take care of you at home? I'm so sorry, I didn't know. That decision is the one I regret making. I wish Mike had been home, he would have known what to do.

9 A.M. The ambulance arrived. Jim was almost rigid, afraid, when the driver and Chris and Heather lifted him onto the stretcher. Jim kept screaming he was going into the wall. Once he was in the ambulance, I got into the ambulance with him, sat next to him, holding his hand, caressing his face, his hair, his body. He, again, was so confused, "What did I do?" Over and over and over.

Repeatedly, I could only say, "Nothing, you did nothing. You will be ok. You did nothing."

Again, "What did I do?"

9:30 A.M. We get to the center. Chris and Heather are right behind. A call to my best friend, Ginny, and she is there in no time. A nurse comes in, says she'll put in buttons to carry all of his medications into his body so he is unafraid and peaceful. Then he can go home in a few days, maybe sooner.

10 A.M. Chris and Heather leave and go to their jobs.

11:30 A.M. The doctor comes, examines him, turns to me and says, "His systems are shutting down, he may die today."

What? He won't come home?

"He may live a few more days, but he won't leave here."

I cannot believe what I've just heard until I look at Jim. I see his mouth open, eyes closed. He is unresponsive, no voluntary movements. I realize he is probably in a coma.

I hold onto him, caress him, hold his hand, talk to him, repeating over and over and over, I love you.

I love you, Jim Danowski.

11:45 A.M. My love, my husband, my life, how will I go on without you? I will miss you so much. I can't in my wildest imagination know how it will be without you.

12 P.M. I glance to my left near the ceiling. There in the corner of the room, something has caught my attention. *The third one, the third one, the third one* . . . I realize it is our third son, Baby Michael, who I miscarried in 1965. I know it is him, and I tell him, "You can't have your daddy yet, Baby Michael. Not yet. We need him a little longer."

Chris and Heather have come back. I begin to tell them about Baby Michael's visit. But before I can say anything, they look at each other and smile. Chris says, "I saw him, Mom, I saw my brother. He was here."

12:30 P.M. Jim's sister, Jan, and her husband, Al, get here. Chris goes to get Mike.

3:15 P.M. After several restless bouts and meds to calm him, an outburst, "Am I going back? Am I going back, Bon? Am I going back?" Then "I'm going back. I'm going back," over and over and over.

"Yes, you are going back home," I tell him, "going back home where you will be safe, be with your folks, all the people who have gone before." This continues.

Suddenly, he says, "I love you. I'm falling, I'm falling, I'm falling."

"No, you are safe. But if you do fall, Mom and Dad are there to catch you," I name as many people as I can think of who have gone before.

His expression changes from distress to peace and he says, "It's beautiful, a few more feet, a few more feet, a few more feet."

We tell him it's ok for him to go. I can tell Mike isn't ready to let his dad go yet. And that's ok.

I ask Jim's mom and dad to come and get him, but he won't go with them.

I can feel all of the ones who went through the veil before in this room. They are all waiting for him, the room is filled with angels—hovering, blessing, being with him, and with us.

I think this was his most evident traveling and returning. Some call it hallucinations, people of faith call it traveling through the veil and back, not quite ready to stay on the other side, not yet. More to do . . .

4:30 P.M. The word is out that Jim won't live much longer. Friends and more family members have come, someone always at his side.

I run home to get clothes, etc. And come right back to stay until the end.

7 P.M. Heather rubs his feet, sending energy and blessing over his body, then crawls under a blanket with Chris on the floor. They smile at each other and hold tight.

Tamara tells Gerry's children that Jim is dying, and the little one, 7 or 8 years old, immediately begins to make a picture. Of course, it is a heart, and inside she prints, "Take me back."

Jim: "Am I going back, Bon?" The picture is synchronicity at its best, I think.

10:45 P.M. Everyone has gone home. I sit by his bed throughout the night, my head on a pillow next to him. I talk to him, sing to him, touch him, reassure him of my love, and tell him I'm sorry I can't make it better.

His breathing is now rattly and erratic. Sometimes I count 3, sometimes 17 between breaths. It's hard for him to breathe, he is working so hard. His heart is strong to keep him going. I doze and wake and cry and want him well again and then want his death to come so he can be free.

September 3—Tuesday

7 A.M. Jan and Al come back. They tell me to sleep, they'll keep watch. I argue but lie down for about 20 minutes, still counting the seconds between his breaths: 3, 10, 4, 17, 5, 3, 6 . . .

I call Jim's brother, Jerry, and ask him to come. Jim would want him here—they love each other so much. Ginny is back, Chris, Heather, Mike all come back.

12 P.M. Two of my performance friends come and sing songs for Jim.

Jan is here. She watches Jim closely. The moment his foot begins to twitch, she knows it's the beginning of full body tremors. She rushes to the nurse's station asking for sedation for him.

Mike and I swab his mouth. I slip in some ice chips, one time he closed his mouth on my fingers. He was always thirsty, why would now be different? I regret not keeping his mouth more moist these days.

Again, forgive me, Jim. I'm sorry.

1:30 P.M. Chris tells me he has ordered the cremains box from the New Mallery Monastery (near my hometown) in Iowa. It is handmade, beautiful, as it should be, oak, engraved with, "The world is a better place because you were here."

It still seems surreal. I pray a lot, asking for courage, asking for Jim to be at peace, for him to know I love him.

My good friend Luis, a Franciscan Friar, had come yesterday and comes again today. Today he gives Jim the sacrament of the sick. He hugs us both. I can see he is crying for us.

2:30 P.M. I had found a beautiful song by Jan Phillips called "Lullabye." It describes holding someone who is dying, as angels sing. I held him softly as we listened to the song together.

His breathing remains erratic all day. Comfort meds every couple of hours.

4 P.M. A harpist comes and plays many of Jim's favorites. He is quiet today.

5:30 P.M. We are thinking maybe Jim wants to talk with his older brother, Ed, and sister, Judy. So Jan has called Ed, put the phone to Jim's ear, and Ed is able to say goodbye.

Then a call to Judy and as it ends, a tear falls from Jim's right eye. Now, we are reassured Jim knows we are here, that he can hear all the love in the room, and knows it is for him.

10 P.M. Everybody leaves after I promise to keep them posted.

10:15 P.M. The nurses say they'll fix the corner sofa into a bed for me. I say, "No, I'm sleeping with Jim tonight." They wash him, make room for me, add a pillow, and I crawl in. His breathing slows to a regular rhythm, still raspy, but he is calmer now.

I say, as we have for so many years, "Good night, I love you, God bless you, see you in the morning."

My head next to his, I talk to him, sing songs, tell stories, and sleep.

September 4—Wednesday

7 A.M. Waking a little after 7 a.m., I am pretty sure this will be our last day.

7:20 A.M. "Baby Michael, it is time. Come get your daddy," I say confidently.

7:35 A.M. Jerry is here, Ginny is here. Ginny shows me a photo of the rainbow she saw on the way to the hospice.

A rainbow makes a promise: we will never be left alone.

We all sit now for a while. His breaths seem further apart.

7:45 A.M. Jim exhales. We wait for the inhale. When there is none, we know he has taken his last breath. Baby Michael has taken his daddy's hand and walked him through the thin veil.

He has left his weary, worn, wounded body, his spirit filled with light and beauty. He is free.

I hold him, my tears bathing his face, filled with love and loss. But—*he is free!*

Jerry calls the nurses.

Bonnie & Jim—Aug. 22, 1964

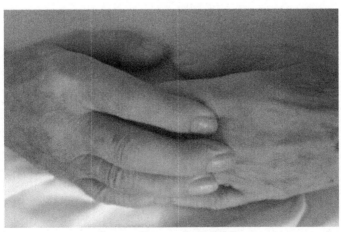

Jim—Sept. 4, 2013

Chapter 8

She Said, He Said, Mostly She Said

THE DAY THEY LOST MY HUSBAND

My husband of 49 years, James G. Danowski, died at 7:45 a.m. on September 4, 2013. We had both signed on with the Donor Network and then a science research facility. Thinking it was a way to pay back for all the gifts that had been in our lives, we had gladly signed the papers to donate our bodies to science.

On the morning that Jim took his last breath, as I held him and told him I loved him one more time and called our sons and other family and friends, I began to prepare for the next step. Being the practical, insane person that I am, after about an hour or so, I called the researchers to come for him. The response I received from the person who answered the phone was first of all, "We are sorry for your loss." Then, "Let me check to see if we can use your husband." I'm told now by family and friends who were there that it was nearly a half hour on hold for them to make the decision, and in the end, yes, they said they would come for him. It must have been a long way, or perhaps they were giving us more time with Jim, since this would be the last time we would be with him. At least an hour and a half later, they came. The departure was gentle and compassionate, and I knew that he was in good hands.

Fast-forward to September 17, when I got a call telling me that his cremains would be here in one to three days. As the evening of the 20th approached and he hadn't shown up, I decided I'd better check on his whereabouts. The lovely young woman who answered the phone looked and looked. I could tell she couldn't find him. Their records showed he had been delivered on the 18th. Whoops! Delivered? Yes, my husband was coming home in the mail truck. And obviously, I hadn't been home, or I'd have him, according to this nice woman. And didn't I have a little orange card stuck in my door telling me they had tried to deliver a package and that it was waiting at the closest post office?

No, I didn't have either my husband or a little orange card. Unaware of which post office they considered to be the closest to me, I asked where to go to pick him up. I also expressed my dismay at the disrespect being shown to my husband's cremains. Couldn't they, in the very least, have had someone bring him home? I mean—the mail? Now, really, that is bizarre. I was told that we could do a "Return to Sender," which would take 14 days, and then I could come get him. Really, you have got to be kidding!

By then, I was in total disbelief, and a little angry too. I was determined to call back during business hours, set an appointment with the CEO and make a personal visit. This is just wrong. This should not be happening, and should never happen to anyone again.

But, it was 5:30 p.m., and there was nothing I could do except check the post office hours and plan to get Jim the next morning.

Come the next morning, Saturday, I reluctantly and nervously showed up at the post office.

"I believe there is a package here for me."

"Name, address, please, let me look." After awhile, "No, nothing back there, do you have a tracking number?"

"No, but I can get it."

Another phone call, the results being a second kind young woman, who also said Jim had been delivered. I'm thinking, well, he's out there somewhere, doing God knows what. She did have the tracking number. Yes, he should be there—he was mailed, it showed him delivered the 18th, but the report was incomplete. What does that mean?

So, back to the agent I went, tracking number in hand. He's here, or so I'm told. The agent went to check.

I'm sure someone has lost my husband. By then, the lines of people were getting longer as I'm holding up both agents who were working that morning. Maybe Jim has gone missing, either near a Wisconsin lake, maybe a beach, or possibly a mountain stream.

Fifteen minutes later, the agent returned. The supervisor found him—on the mail truck! For delivery today. Just be sure to get home so I don't miss him and have to come back on Monday to get him. Rushing out and jumping into my Escape, I had to get home or he'd go missing again.

At noon, there I was at my desk looking out the window at the mailbox. Obviously, Jim was riding around the neighborhood. I wondered if he had convinced the driver to stop at any of the yard sales along the way, and perhaps, just perhaps, that was why he hadn't shown up yet? You'd have to know how much he loved to peruse the neighborhood looking for those garage sale signs.

Finally, Jim is home, safely delivered! He is resting comfortably in a beautiful oak box that has been handmade by the New Mallery, Iowa, Trappist Monks, never to be lost again. I promise, my love, I promise.

HE ALWAYS SAID HE'D BE WATCHING

I've heard it said by many wise prophets and some wee-bit-crazed folks that when we leave this world, we sometimes come back to complete what we may have started. Maybe because we weren't quite ready to go, or we have more things to say, to do, more loving to do, maybe. Sometimes the strings to those still left here are not broken, and we're called back. I don't know about any of that. What I do believe, though, is that this world and the ones beyond are terribly close, if not totally overlapping, and easy to cross—especially when the ties are so very strong.

Call me crazy, but I know that is what happened after Jim left. Following are some of my remembrances.

September 4, 2013—about 8:15 A.M.

James Gerard Danowski had exhaled his last breath and his spirit soared into eternity. Eyes closed, mouth agape. About ten minutes later, after talking with the doctor, I turned back to look at this man I'd shared the majority of my life with. I saw peace and freedom on his face. His lips were closed and formed the smile I remembered seeing when he knew all was good. Not possible, you say? Ah, but I was there. Everyone there saw him too, and we knew he was okay—and we would be too.

September 5, 6 & 7

Jim's power chair sat in the utility room. For the three days following his death, the toggle switch was turned on. I turned it off each day, but the next morning, it was back on again.

September 5

Jim used to have a banana every morning with his cereal. Our son, Chris, was vacuuming his house, and he'd had a banana for breakfast. He came across the little black bitter end of the banana that no one eats in the corner of the living room. He thinks, "Hm, I don't remember dropping it!" Before finishing his cleaning, he found two more fresh black banana tips in two more rooms.

September 8

The white dove I had seen for 2 or 3 days before Jim died returned. A sign of peace, hope and life, I thought.

September 11—9:07 A.M.

The house needed a cleaning, so I got out the vacuum cleaner. I was waiting for a call from the insurance adjuster, since the roof was leaking, so I put my phone in my pocket just in case he would call. Suddenly in the middle of the family room, I heard something very loud. Turning off the vacuum. I realized the sound was Tune-In Radio, which could only be accessed through the music app (I hadn't done that). A group called Train singing "Calling All Angels" was at the highest volume on the phone. The Beach Boys followed them with "How Do You Mend a Broken Heart?" I asked Jim how long this private concert was going to last! The station went to commercial.

September 13

I was on my way to meet up with this group of women I call "my women's circle" in the White Mountains. Somewhere between Pinetop and Greer, I was in that place where you're not awake but not asleep either (don't worry, my friend was driving). I heard Jim: "I'm ok, I'm ok, Bon."

September 14—2 A.M.

At Diane's house in Greer. Ginny saw the door to my bedroom was open after I went to bed, later it was closed. I was asleep. Who else was there?

September 14

During the last few months of Jim's life, we had started to playfully read our horoscopes each morning. I checked Jim's that day. It read: "The overriding feeling is that you're on your way. Where to? Does that really matter at this ripe moment of fresh optimism? Use your happy feet and go forth with gusto."

September 18

T3, my son Mike's beagle, began howling around midnight—a mournful howl, on the patio, and in the kitchen. He was unconsolable. Mourning? I waited and watched with him on the patio from 2:45 to 3:45 a.m. until he was peaceful again.

September 19

A Google calendar message: "JMGD@ gmail.com: remove from calendar." Then "JimDanowski@gmail.com: remove from calendar."

September 20

Phone reminder came up on my phone: Jim see Dr. Bruce.

September 29

Mass at the Casa. The reading happened to be the same scripture that had been chosen for Jim's memorial service on the 27th, a few days earlier:

"But godliness with contentment is great gain. For we brought nothing into the world, and we can take nothing out of it. But if we have food and clothing, we will be content with that . . . But you, man of God, flee from all this, and pursue righteousness, godliness, faith, love, endurance and gentleness" (1 Tim. 6:6-8 & 11).

September 29

Later that same night, a dream: Jim walked through the front door, "Where are my magazines?" he said. I told him most of them had expired. (I had called all of the magazines to stop delivery a week ago.) He lay down on the couch, and in my dream I knew he realized he was going to die soon. He closed his eyes and was quiet.

September 30

I went into the office early to start working. When I tried to print, I looked at the power strip, and the printer was unplugged.

October 4

Again in my office, the lamp on my desk was unplugged from the power strip.

October 6

My son Mike had a dream that we were in the Ford Escape, but he didn't know where we were going. I was driving, he was in the back, and Jim was in the passenger seat, the way it always was. At one point, Jim turned to look at Mike, gently waved and quietly said, "Bye." Mike didn't understand what it meant in the dream, but when he woke, he knew his dad had come to see him.

October 27

Another message from Jim, "It'll be ok, Bon, it'll be ok." The phrase had changed from "I'm ok," to "It's ok," to this. Maybe he was telling me to not expect a quick resolution or clarity on anything.

Or maybe all of these messages were just what they were, and shouldn't be analyzed. Maybe they were only to make me aware he was closeby. Let God be God.

October 30, 2013—4:14 A.M.

Dana Point, CA. I'd taken a quick trip to the ocean to soothe my soul. I'd been up since 2 a.m., just to hear waves unencumbered by traffic and trains. I turned on Pandora, and it began playing an instrumental, "The Ocean Blue." I didn't think much about it, but next came "Out of the Darkness," which was what my writing at 2 a.m. had been all about. The third selection was called "Listening to the Heart." All I could say was thank you, Creator Universal Mystery, and Jim.

January 18, 2014

I hadn't written for awhile. I didn't know why—I guess, I hadn't had any messages. That morning, though, I heard Jim, loud and clear: "You don't need me anymore."

It nearly broke my heart. I cried through the morning. It felt like a final goodbye—I knew the kids needed him, so maybe that was what he was focused on instead of me. Maybe it meant that our relationship was changing to one of just checking in, just being aware. Maybe it was his way of setting me free, to trust myself, to be confident in what I would do, my decisions, how I lived. If that was the case, it was probably a very positive thing. I wished I'd known for certain.

Once again, I turned this over to Divine Mystery and knew that the resolution was already there, that I would understand in due time, to be patient, to trust in my history that I had never been alone and wouldn't ever be.

September 3-4, 2016

Lake Arrowhead. The weekend when Jim left—three years ago. Something always seemed missing. It felt like I was always forgetting something when I left or returned to the house. He was still here, just in a different form. It was a new way of being and seeing. I could see him, holding me in the backyard. Where did that picture go anyway?

I had this card called "Five Ways Messages Come From The Other Side: butterflies, coins, unexpected music, familiar aromas, feathers." I found them all that day—a little yellow butterfly on a flowering plant, coin underfoot, "What a Wonderful World" on the town square speaker, Irish Spring soap on the store counter. Only one was missing: feathers.

I'd been looking down as I walked the path near the lake. Surely, there was a feather somewhere.

I was prompted to look skyward. First one—two, no, three—then four eagles flew overhead and across the lake. Magnificent!

Thank you, Jim, you never did do mediocre things. I love you.

September 26, 2016

Semi-awakened early in the morning. Was someone here? Who was standing trancelike in front of the green chair and ottoman in the corner of my bedroom? A young man, dark hair, transparent—only part of him, a spirit? Then it transformed into Jim, beard, dark hair, again transparent as a ghost. My brain and will wanted to see more, to make the figure clearer. Just like that, he was gone . . .

He's here again

Jim has been showing up this month in strange and different ways. Oftentimes in the music on Pandora, with our favorite songs that always point me to him: "The Wedding Song," "Bridge Over Troubled Waters," "In the Misty Moonlight," "The Top of the World."

Things seem to be missing and suddenly, there they are, though I know I'd looked there before.

Last month, he was busy around his birthday. I saw three vans just like ours, all on the same day, though I haven't seen any like it since selling it over a year ago.

Then one morning I awoke. I had had the outside door open, so it was cold in my room. I looked up, and the ceiling fan was on. He always slept with it on. The next morning, same thing. There is no way I could have turned it on without knowing it, since I would have had to reach around the back of the bed frame to do it.

It had to be him.

CONVERSATIONS

October 26, 2013

It is past midnight by the sea. Healing waves ebb and flow, carrying in and carrying out the beach sand that I love to walk on. The waves are beautiful, life-giving, and deadly. The power in those waves has the potential to give life—and the power to take life.

I sometimes feel as if I'm in a bricked up building that he can pass through, but only with help from those who know the way, for they've done it before. I told him I'd be okay, today I'm not so sure.

Is it possible to hold contradictions like this as equal yet in opposition? Is it the way of life? The sun sends life-giving rays. The sun's rays burn and kill. The rain gives life-giving water. The rain drowns. It is the way—birthing, living, dying.

"In God's time," the elders say. Trust, believe, understand. I marvel at this thing called life. One day we are born, we are here, then we aren't. One day, he was here, then he wasn't. One day he laughed, told stories, delighted in his family. Then he didn't. One day his heart beat, then it stopped. He exhaled a breath, and his life went with it. He needed me to be with him till the end. I was.

October 30

On the beach, at Dana Point. I guess now I know how it is without you. You were my anchor—to reality, to who I am, to life itself. I feel like a rowboat on a big ocean without a compass. I'm scared out here. It's fine when the sun is shining.

What about when the storms come? How will I stay afloat? Will I sink? Will I get lost forever to the whimsy of the currents and waves?

What about nighttimes when it's dark and I can't find the lighthouse. What then? Where will my strength come from?

Suddenly, Jim is here: "Look to your God, Bon. You won't be abandoned. That's a promise, remember."

I'm not sure I do.

"You know what to do—get back to your contemplative prayer practice. Get back in touch with the Creator, who is always holding you."

I know. You are right about that. But why do I feel so lost? Because of your illness, we've led fairly parallel lives for years. You'd think I'd be more together.

"Who are you kidding? We were together nearly 50 years. Sure, you're lost. But I'm close. I'm watching. Want me to put in a word with the Universe for you?"

That would help. And to open my heart to hear and to know God is near and watching out for me—and our sons Mike and Chris too.

"I'll talk to them. I'm glad you went to the ocean. It's good for you, I know that. Sorry I couldn't go with you."

Me too. Wasn't our life together grand! We did okay, you and I. I think we did. What now? I want to be more comfortable with who I am. I wonder if I'll ever be the best me there is.

"Bon, you know better. You are beautiful, good, unselfish, smart, gifted. I liked the way, when you were going out the door, you would ask me if you looked fat, were you smart enough, or would you give a good talk.

So silly. You were my life too, you know. Know I am so proud of you. I always have been."

So I start this next chapter alone. Enjoy your new life, husband. I did love you.

"I know. I'll be here when you call."

November 4

It is morning now, the waves are high, as they strike the beach, powerful beyond imagination. It's been two months since the morning he exhaled his last breath. A part of me went with him; a part of him remains with me.

I return to the sea seeking solace, as I have so many times before. New life awaits here, in the water, in the air. Here at Dana Point I watch as people walk by.

The sea is restless today. Fog hides the sun, water, sand. My grief is concealed within the same dense, white fog. My fear of what is hidden keeps it there, until its screams demand it be seen.

November 28

Happy Thanksgiving, Jim. My husband, how are you today? How has your new life been for you? It's so different here. Sometimes I cry and cry. You should still be here. For many reasons you should be here.

Your body just couldn't anymore—after so many years of suffering with pain, exhaustion, psoriasis, then the cancer, your fall, and cancer again. You went through so much. I am sorry, husband, I am so sorry you had to suffer so. And you seldom complained.

It is hard, being new to this, you know. I often don't know what to do. We knew each other so well that we would finish each other's sentences. And often we had conversations without words.

Can you believe the pipe behind the washer burst yesterday? Unreal. It's going to cost a thousand—a thousand I certainly didn't have in the budget. You were always so easy with money. Get it, you would say. Get two!

So today is Thanksgiving. You liked this day. You were always happy to have the kids here. I worked my fanny off, you knew it, but couldn't do much about it. I will miss having everyone here today. It's very early, and I miss you. Always as we woke on these days, the first thing was to wish each other Happy Thanksgiving.

So, Happy Thanksgiving. I wonder what your life is really like. What do you do there? Will you be near today? I don't have to ask if you are okay because I know you are, just wondering what it is that you do every day. It isn't fair that you can keep tabs on me and I can't on you.

So be well, husband of mine—fly, come by, talk to me, protect me. Happy Thanksgiving. I miss you.

November 29

Good morning, how are you today? So what was Thanksgiving like for you? Do you have turkey where you are? Mine turned out really good yesterday. It was quite the time at Tam and Gerry's. They did such a great job, so much work with all of the foods. And everyone had so much fun talking and laughing. It was a celebration. I missed you. I know they did too.

I think I will begin Christmas today, get the Santas down, all that. What are you called there? Send me your new name, okay? I love you forever.

January 1, 2014
Good morning, husband. How are you? Chris tells me that you are still in-between? Are you lost, unable to find your way? Can I do anything? Probably not. It is your life, not mine.

I would wish for you all the joy of the next life, as we have always believed. Is it so, or is it myth? Chris says he talks to you, that he sees you wandering, not at peace. You did not want to leave, we all knew that. But your body gave out. Your spirit remained strong. And so today I don't understand your not being peaceful. Stop worrying about me, ok? I am ok. I will be ok. I am so surrounded by friends and family that I know I will be ok.

I miss you though. A lot. I look at your chair and see Corky, not you. This little dog misses you so very much. There is no consoling her. Only you coming home will make her happy again. And that won't happen.

Today I miss you. I do want you home. I want you back, like you were 40 years ago. Not like the last 15 years. The decline became more obvious and steady, and you were never the same again. That's a long time, you know. I was angry with the disease, sometimes with you because you wouldn't or couldn't do what I thought you could.

You are gone. My God assures me I will be taken care of. I must believe and embrace that promise. I think that I do believe.

Have a peaceful, joyful day, Jim. May you find your way soon. I need you to be there for me someday.

January 4

A message from Jim: "I miss you. I love you. I can't wait to see you. You'll be surprised. It's like what we talked about but so much more (endless and endless). Don't worry about the stuff of the world. The material stuff is part of the distraction."

March 4

It's 5:55 a.m., on Tuesday, March 4th—6 months since 7:45 a.m., September 4th. Gone such a short time, gone such a long time.

Where are you? How are you? Have you found someone to talk with? To dance with? To polka with? To understand that marvelous brain of yours? To challenge you? To ride bikes with? To ride with you in the snow, remember?

Are you happy? Most of all, are you happy? Free of pain, free of MS, free, free, free . . .

Why do the ones left behind not feel happy? Why do we grieve? Why is death? Why is parting?

Why did you go? Why not me? Am I not done yet? Were you?

Live on, husband—in all you did here, in all you loved, in all who loved you.

One year later

So this is what it is like, a year later. Lying here at 5 a.m., awake since 3 a.m., wondering, just wondering, where you are, how you are, what you are doing. Will we find each other again sometime? What will that be like? Have you found everyone? Your folks, mine, Baby Michael, Tony, John, all of your old Cursillo guys. Aunts, grandparents, uncles, my family, what do you think? They were interesting. Does Grandma Kate still dislike your beard? Do you still have it? How old are you? Do you age there? Are you well?

Do we come back to this world again? Neither you nor I wanted to, do you remember? We figured one time was sufficient! We just hoped to return to whoever and wherever we came from.

WEDNESDAY IN BERLIN

I sit in this park in the center of Berlin. I can only wonder how this has come about. How is it that one year ago on this day, July 24th, I was taking care of my husband. He was evaporating before my eyes as the cancer was growing inside of him; 42 days later, he would be gone.

In this trip to Europe of 35 days, I have traveled by plane, train, bus, and car to cities and through countrysides in seven countries. What an incredible world we live in. How blessed am I to be here. I have traveled far.

These many miles have been filled with delight. My travel companions and I added our bows to the fairy trees in Ireland. We wondered at the little yellow flowers that grew through the snow of a mountaintop in Switzerland. In Prague, we were amazed to see the castle that overlooked the city, near the Jewish cemetery where bodies were buried in a 20-foot mound. We found curiosity in Stonehenge, where large stone formations were created many centuries ago. We were astonished with disbelief as we walked through the Sachsenhausen Concentration Camp near Berlin. This must never happen again! I prayed at the border between the original city of Dresden and the bombed section.

Yet, in the last 42 days of Jim's life, I had traveled farther than I could ever have imagined. He and I walked hand-in-hand in that journey too, knowing our life together was ending, and wanting to live every day just loving each other. I didn't know the end of that journey, where he would go. One morning he left, gone like the sun at sunset, the moon at sunrise—gone—except the sun and the moon come back.

This journey will end in five days, and I'll go home.

Yellow flowers with snow in Switzerland

I LOVE YOU STILL

Ache
Broken
Alone
Lonely

You're not coming back
Are you?
Left too soon
Those final days
Too quick

Too much to understand
Too much for my heart
Torn away from us
You didn't want to go
It was so hard for you
Not resigned to dying
Fought to the end

Did you find peace?
Not peaceful those last days
I couldn't fix it
So sorry
Couldn't console you
Even as I held you
Through the day and night

At last on Wednesday morning
You couldn't will yourself to live anymore
You exhaled a final breath

We waited and there was nothing
Your spirit, your life had changed
At that moment
The you we understood had gone away

I love you still, husband,
I hope you are happy, filled with the joy
You so deserve, peaceful and celebrating
Your spirit is near
Always

30,000 FEET

30,000 feet or so in the air
3/4 of the way to my destination
I remember
Do you
So many years ago

Coming home
High above the clouds
There was music in those days
Coming from the speakers
Carpenters singing "The Top of the World"

We were, you and I
So long ago now
I miss you, husband
I love you
I remember us

How are you these days
Where are you
Are you near

I am okay.
Your last message was
It will be okay
It will, I know it will

It is, husband.
It is.

Chapter 9

Looking Back,
Looking Ahead

BROKEN

Universal mystery
Ragged edges in my heart
Sharp, jagged, cutting

As an ornament
Fallen to the floor
Once whole, now in pieces

Takes the master to make it whole again
Broken, mended, stronger
Not as beautiful with its cracks

But stronger
Don't drop it again
Please

CHRISTMASTIME

My heart hurts
Heartbreak is real
Pain so deep
Emptiness
Tears roll

Gone
He is gone
Near yes
Yet far

Lonely alone
Everywhere
In silence
In crowds
In community

It is so
For now

THE BATTLE IS DONE

The yellow rays of the bright sun
Shine, illuminate this small statue
A proud warrior and his loyal horse
The battle over
They've come home
Prepared to die

The warrior, limp in his saddle
His horse, head dropping to the ground
Both home
Heroes, each, fought the fight
Now finished

There is dignity in that pose
Though injured, even beaten
Time to move on
To a brighter place
Where new life begins
Again

A RING

I fill out forms that say single
A ring on my finger
Says I'm married
I'm not

I was once
No more
Death does that
Till death we promised

So, now what?
The ring—a lie?
The ring—a symbol?
No more?

Transformed
More than marriage
We were as one
United

In death
Like not before
Whole as one
Now changed

It's cold out there
Cold in here
Without him
I hope he's warm

HUSBAND, YOU KNOW

Husband, you know
Don't you?
All is well, isn't it?
Live in Spirit
Abide there
Be well
The tent of solitude
Be at home there

I have prepared a place for you
A magnificent place
You will see
When it is time
Not now, my love, not now

BUTTERFLY

The cycle goes on
The caterpillar shed its simple shell
A miracle, the butterfly emerged
Tested its wings
And flew

He too, shed his simple human shell
A miracle, transformed in beauty
He flew away
Leapt into eternity
Gone for now
Absorbed into the ethos

It's not so hard
When we believe
As each chrysalis bursts open
A new life emerges
A life eternal, forever

The shell is shed
Transformed now
The breath is new
Filled with the grace
Of the Creator
Complete

ONE DAY

Remember me
I remember you
I see you in the stars
Shining bright in the night sky
You shine more brightly now

We shall meet again
In lush meadows and fields
On the tallest mountain
And the deepest valley
Near the oceans and rivers and streams
And in the bare desert

One day we will hold each other
And dance above the clouds
Fly with eagles
And swim beneath the sea
To play with dolphins
One day

For now I see you in the stars
Shining bright in the night sky
You shine most brightly
On the darkest nights

Not yet
But
One day

SHOES

Shoes beneath the window
His shoes
Maybe mine too someday
Not yet, not yet

Too many more miles to go
Shoes for walking
Shoes for dancing, spinning in the sand
Flying through the air, keeping time
Always keeping time

Shoes for climbing mountains
As yet unseen
We did those things, he and I
Often only in our dreams
Shoes for resting in my easy chair

Shoes that took us to the center
And all around.
Together we were
And we are
Traveling near, now far

New shoes for him
New shoes for me?
To travel on
Him and me

Someday?

FLY

The eagle sits by herself
Safely in the nest
She had shared with her mate
For a long time

So in love
They were
Alone now
She remembers

He'd fly away
Always returning
Bringing her a gift
A twig for their nest

Food for the day
Sometimes surprises
A piece of a rainbow
A rose petal sweet

In the times
When her soul felt lost
They would fly to the sea
To bathe in its waters

They soared side by side
Above the arid desert
Mountains covered with grasses
Or winter snow
To the life-giving sea

Her soul restored
Their flight home, ah,
How free, delightful
Diving, soaring, playing in the winds
Alive again, whole again

She sits now
Alone
High above the world
That once was

She saw him fly
That last time
Reluctant to leave
His wings not strong
His body tired

Called to another reality
Slowly stretching his wings
He lifted his pain-filled body
Caught an air current
Relinquished his power

As he let go
He glowed
Filled with a new light
His wings his body his soul
Becoming one with the sky

He flew as never before
Higher and higher
Further and further

Soon gone
Transformed. Free
His memory remains
Alone now in their nest
Her spirit broken
She sits and waits

Once again
The sea calls
To restore
Her shattered soul
To wholeness

She answers
As she knows she must
Finding the wind
Her wings unfold

High above the clouds
She flies to the sea
And she says "Yes"
It is good to be alive.

IV

YES, THIS IS MY PATH

The winds of change blow hard.
I resisted them with my whole being,
then I learned to tolerate them.
Finally, I can embrace them.
That has changed my life.

CHAPTER 10

Gifts Along the Way

BROKEN & BEAUTIFUL

A couple of weeks ago I spent a few days in Rocky Point with friends. As I walked on the sand at the edge of the Sea of Cortez, I could see all around me on the shore sea shells of different sizes, shapes, colors. I found a sand dollar, perfectly formed and whole. My friend said when these beautiful little shells are broken open, there's an even more beautiful surprise inside. But we can't see it until the shell is broken. Once it breaks, we discover the twists, spirals and surprises created in nature and through the Creator's playful side.

But wait, there's more: within the sand dollar, once broken, are found tiny, identical doves, formed by the sand having settled into the crevices. Indeed, the Creator is magnificent, waiting for us to find so many surprises in each day.

If there is such beauty in a broken sea shell, is there not beauty in our brokenness? Could it be when we are dashed against the rocks by the daily surf of life, as the sea creatures are, sometimes a part of us breaks.

John Duns Scotus, a thirteenth-century Scottish Franciscan theologian, wrote extensively on the connectedness and individuality of everyone. He taught that brokenness in ourselves is the only way that we can see the brokenness in others. St. Francis and Jesus saw the beauty in the broken people of their times, the leper, the poor, the marginalized.

It is in this brokenness that what we have had hidden breaks out. We see things differently, perhaps. When we find our dependence on the Creator's love, we can see that we're no different from the rest of creation, often broken, healed, broken. Beautiful because we are loved. Simple as that.

The Divine Healer calls, "Come to me . . . and I will give you rest" (Matt. 11:28). Our brokenness can be patched together, and make us stronger and more beautiful than before. The Divine All gives us comfort and gifts us with compassion, empathy, and love for others who walk this often rocky journey.

Our faith tells us we are held securely in our Creator's unconditional love, accepting us as we are, breathing life into us, healing our brokenness. It is then that we can hear that still small voice within telling us, "Just do the next right thing. You are loved and safe in the palm of my hand. You are home. You are meant to live and love and know brokenness as Jesus did and still carry on. Be broken and be beautiful."

The beauty we see within the cast away seashell
Teaches us to open our minds and hearts
To that tiny voice within
That urges us to welcome our brokenness
And our beauty
To know we are truly wonderfully made.

We seek the wisdom
To hear and to follow
The soft and tender inner voice
Constantly calling us
To be still,
To be quiet,

To take heart
To find the courage
To see the beauty in the broken.

As we remember Jesus
His brokenness
taken to The Divine Healer, his Abba,
We dare to listen in stillness
To that tiny voice deep within,
"Come to me.
In your brokenness, you
Will know the beautiful."

Sand dollar, broken open

ANOTHER CHRISTMAS

I watch out my window
Caught by surprise
Ten parakeets on the saguaro
They like to nest in the cactus

The cactus wren does not approve
So the little green birds return
To their second best nest
In a mesquite down the street

I too dream of a better home
This, my home of 45 years
It's modest, safe, comfortable
Filled with so many memories

Today, Christmas Eve,
As each year comes, I remember
Mike with his music, Chris and theater
Jim and his love for us

So much unpredictability
Most of those years
Simpler today, it seems
I know so much more

My directive is clear:
Be fair, be merciful
Be humble, walk with God
I think I'll stay

BABIES AWAKEN

The darkness has gone
Replaced by the light of day
Now I see
More clearly

I hear the sounds of nature
Outside my window
The birds are awake now
Babies in the over-stuffed birdhouse
Hanging in the olive tree

Peeking out, chirping
No, summoning
The adults to feed them,
Their soft yellow beaks
Popping out as so many others
Over these nearly 20 years

Then the sound of the hawk
Sitting at the top of Grandfather Pine
Calling for his mate
A harsh signal for all to heed

The air is filled with noisy chatter
Warning sounds to the babies
Of the smaller winged ones
Stay hidden. Don't venture out.
It is not safe.

The hawk spots his mate

Stretches his wings
Hurls himself into the air
And flies over my home

The little winged ones emerge
From their hiding places
Safe once again

The day ripens with sunlight
White clouds float in the blue skies
and all is well again

THE PITCHER

An old pitcher
A lovely pitcher used and worn
The once ornate pattern faded
Showing the years

Once a sparkling new
Piece of porcelain
Sits empty
On a shelf

The once fragrant healing elixir
Poured out
Gone
Empty, not a solitary drop remained

The now empty container,
Once filled to the brim, now used up
Living does that

This faded pitcher sits
Waits
To be tossed away?
To hold a new elixir?

It waits
On a shelf
Silently, quietly, ever vigilant
It can do nothing less
Nothing more, nothing else

An old faded pitcher
Trusting the tender Mystery
That holds all
It waits, waits
And waits.

SUCH GIFTS ARE OURS

This morning, such magnificence
Looking to the sky, a new sound
Coming into sight above my trees
A pair of eagles, so beautiful

They talk a lot to each other
I didn't know that
Gracefully lighting in Grandfather Pine
All the while chattering

A brief moment, too brief
Then they flew over the trees
Into the clouds
It is spring, the winged ones know

Yesterday a quail on my window ledge
What will the morrow bring
It doesn't matter really
Today was enough

UP EARLY

Up early with the workers of the earth
Morning is such a good time
The transition time from dark to light
From cold to warm
From asleep to awake

The trees welcome the day
With arms outstretched
Ready to receive the sunlight
And give praise

The animals waken, stretch,
Blink and look for a caress
To tell them they are loved
And appreciated

The birds sing their songs
To their Maker and glorify
God with their beauty
And uniqueness
Then they go off to care
For their families

The caterpillars come up from the
Warm home they have burrowed
Into hiding places as they grow and grow
Into the time when wings sprout
And fly away

Metamorphosis, like life, does not end

But changes and reaches higher
Levels—all in the Maker's plan

The evolution continues
And creation moans and squeals
Alternately as everyone and everything
Changes and reaches new heights

GEODES

A new-found rock
Creamy color
Rough just a rock
Like all of the others

Tap it, wait
No sound comes back
Just an ordinary rock
Among so many

Explore further
They say there is more
Explore the crevices
It's just a rock

Then the wise ones
Say go deeper
Deeper?
But it's just a rock

Deep within its center
Awaits a treasure
Like no other
How?

Break it open
But then it is broken
Yes, but—
Open and see

Broken open
Within this ordinary shell
Find brilliant crystals
Shining in the sun

Crystals laughing, sparkling
Awakened now
Released from darkness
Hidden in an ordinary rock

Oh what treasures
Beauty
Brilliance
Lie hidden within

BLESSING

Bless You, Wondrous Gifter,
For another day
At the Source

Sea, sand, sky,
The beginning, over and over
The beginning—
Each moment

Close to the first day of creation
When You said, "Let it be"
And it was good

And it is good

A BLANK PAGE

A blank page before me. What to do with it? A poem, story, picture, theory, nonsense.

Something must be worth writing. At age 77, I realize that I have lived more years than I have yet to live. It isn't the years that are important. It is how I have lived them. My whole being tells me there are many more things to experience in the next years. Surely, a gift, isn't it? My mother died at 68. She missed so much. Three short months ago, my little brother died at 73. A restless and adventurous wanderer, he left a legacy of love and fairness for all of us who knew him.

In this imperfect world, filled with contradictions and conundrums, we humans go from day to day, often stumbling in the dark. Then, if we're lucky, someone reaches out a hand to help us along.

It has been that way for me. I see it in all of the incredibly gifted, loving people who have invited me into their lives, the animals who have loved me, even strangers. It tells me that all of creation is connected. We all share the same air, the same earth, we all want to be happy and to do something, anything, that leaves a mark, that tells those who follow that we were here.

Let's make things a little better, a little less difficult. Be compassionate. Don't judge. Do love. Don't criticize. Do compliment. Don't hate. Do love. Don't hurt. Do good. Don't break. Do mend. Don't cry too often. Do laugh a lot. Don't worry. Do trust.

The Eternal One, filled with all good, love, compassion, wisdom, cares for all. Loves all, holds all, laughs with all, cries with all. The Eternal One waits and waits for us to call out, to reach out, to welcome that power and love into our lives, to be engulfed by this eternal love that never quits.

I live each day believing the words of Julian of Norwich six centuries ago, "All shall be well. And all shall be well. And all manner of things shall be well."

So it is...

FLY AWAY

There is a God-given dignity in every living thing, and all that appear to be non-living things. That is what creates and charges all power.

Power comes from Divine Mystery. It dwells within and surrounds all of us. The power within is enhanced through the connectedness of everything, alive or dead to this life. I think maybe the more we connect with the life force of all, the more power is within. How does that power surrounding us manifest itself?

It is like a helium-filled balloon, which rises and floats in the air under its own power. When picked up by a breeze, it rises higher and higher. When picked up by the power of a hurricane, it soars into the atmosphere. So much more exciting—and frightening. Does it stay tied to one place, never to go further, never to experience true freedom, never to float over the mountains, canyons, streams and oceans, never to soar with angels, risk being broken before its time? Or does it remain anchored and safe?

There is only so much helium, only so much time. The helium determines when it will no longer be airborne. So too with us. Do we stay anchored? Or do we trust the Universal Power all around us? Do we believe that it truly will carry us to heights never imagined, never dreamed possible?

Reach out, breathe in that Mystery power, and fly. Be free. That is my choice.

CHAPTER 11

Growing Up, Growing Older

AN IOWA DAY

The little girl ran frantically down the lane, "Daddy, daddy, take me with you." She fell on the stones, tore her knee, blood trickled out as the pickup sped away. The man, unshaven, a pipe in his mouth, in his overalls, sweat-soaked straw hat, was thinking of the crops.

She lay there on the gravel awhile, winded as much from her yearning to be with her father as from the fall.

From out of nowhere came the big brown lumbering dog her brother had named "Chocolate." As he lay his head next to hers, comforting her as only animals can, she felt better.

Soon she was petting him, and they were walking back to the house yard. It was a warm summer morning, and the peacefulness of this Iowa day began to reach into the child's being. She stopped to catch hold of and swing from a branch of one of the pines in the row lining the lane, as the dog playfully chased her bare, tanned feet.

Jumping down, she ran to the house to ask her mother if she could pick some strawberries from the patch for dinner. Her father would be back by then.

VOWS

I take you as my husband, for better for worse, for richer, for poorer . . . I take you as my wife, for better, for worse, for richer, for poorer, in sickness and in health . . . how many years ago? Long enough that the vows still included that obedience clause. Sheesh, stop reminding me. I had my fingers crossed when I said that part.

Besides, things change, times change. Our lives changed. Remember? Kids—two of them, boys, need I say more? We moved away from family, remember? Times were hard. Our nights out consisted of going to a nice restaurant and ordering a cup of coffee. We could barely afford that. Remember? Finishing school, a new job for you. I stayed with my job at the hospital, remember? We missed our dream vacation, for just the two of us, to Vienna, to sail down the Danube and walk through the castles. Remember? We grew apart and lost each other, went for help and once again found us. Remember?

I take you as my husband, for better, for worse, for richer, for poorer, in sickness and in health. I take you as my wife, for better, for worse, for richer, for poorer, in sickness and in health . . .

Jim & Bonnie

MOTHERHOOD

Motherhood, blissful, beautiful, blessed motherhood. I just keep telling myself that. Hey, he's a teenager. Do I have to say anything more? Puberty, sshmuberty. He's turning into an adult, and I'm turning into a crazy lady. One day he comes home from the mall (I thought that's where he went), hurries to his room, and I don't see him again till dinnertime. When he sits down at the table, he keeps tilting his head to the side. I ask him if he's not feeling well or is his neck stiff or what? He says no, nothing. I ask again. Finally I get up to check his forehead—he's got to have a fever or something.

What did you *do*? There, right under his left ear, is a drawing of a rabbit—a rabbit, for God's sake—a little brown rabbit with black eyes and a pink nose. It'll wash off, won't it? Please tell me it'll wash off. You are grounded, young man, until it wears off. He says it's a permanent tattoo, and I say, tough, you are never leaving the house again. That's that. Now eat your dinner!

TAKE ME OUT TO THE BALL GAME

"Take me out to the ball game. Take me out with the crowd. Buy me some peanuts and Cracker Jack . . . " Do you know that song? It's by Albert Von Tilzer and Jack Norworth. They had no idea what *my* life is like. They couldn't have lived in the middle of the city with a spouse and a couple of kids.

I would love to go to the ball game. It doesn't matter that I'm not that big a fan anymore. Instead, I get up at 5 so I can get my son, Mike, to his early morning swim class, run home, breakfast with son, Chris, then a quick peck on the cheek from my husband as he flies out the door to the safety of his office. Then it's a load of laundry, take the dog for her walk, water the plants I'm trying to keep alive in the middle of this God-awful heat. Why do I bother? I know that come July 27, on schedule, everything wilts and goes to plant heaven, anyway. It happens every year. The phone rings, the carpet I ordered for the family room is backordered. Wipe off the tables, get the mail. By then it's noon, oops, forgot to pick up Mike. Out the door. He's angry and pouts all of the way home.

By the time I get home, Chris needs to go to his summer class. Drive him. Back by 2. What happened to lunch? Forget it. Check the freezer, what will I fix for dinner? The phone rings again, and now Mom says she forgot to ask me to take her to the doctor at 3:30. Of course, I'll take you, I say. Mike is clamoring for the phone to call Kelly to go to the mall. Kelly's mom will take them—there is a God! Pick up Chris, no time to take him home so he goes with me to the doctor with

Mom. Not happily though. Home by 5:30. Dinner, oh my gosh, forgot to thaw something. Call husband—Honey, pick up pizza, okay? 6:45 collapse with the last piece of pizza and a cool glass of chardonnay. Asleep on the couch by 8:30.

Take me out to the ball game. I have a craving for peanuts.

PINE TREES

It was 78 degrees as I sat on the deck of my friend's home in the beautiful northern Arizona White Mountains. I was surrounded by mature, tall, long-needled pine trees that held the familiar childhood smell that I had grown up with. On the farm, there had been a grove of 100-foot-tall pines just north of the house. When the wind blew, which it frequently did in this Iowa valley, the pines sang a song unlike any other.

I hadn't heard that sound for such a long time—how long, exactly, oh my goodness—45 years probably. But this evening, the wind was strong, and the pines sang their magnificent song. Some say the pines whistle and whisper. Their lives are precious and precarious in this arid northern desert. The wind brings the promise of rain in its prelude, and another song will erupt with the rain.

As I anxiously awaited the rain to come, I remembered the nights I used to lie awake in my bed when I was a child, sometimes imagining the pines to be reaching out to hold me tenderly, other times imagining them to be grasping to pull me from my bed.

They were very tall cumbersome pines, not unlike most pines in the northeastern part of Iowa, where farmland was beautiful, black, and fertile. Every farm had pine trees, not just because of their beauty, but mostly because they were a useful windbreak from the northern wind, which was often cruel and filled with ice and snow. Iowa farmers were pragmatic if they were anything. They understood the earth—if they didn't, they didn't make it. My dad understood the earth and all of its gifts and the animals that lived on it. Each living being had its use, each had its uniqueness. Each part reflected God in its own way, so that when all the parts were put together, they created a full picture of the Creator. Saints have names for this, but farmers just know that is the way things work. End of discussion, simple as that. "It just works," my dad would say when I would ask "why."

The Iowa pine trees were alive, very alive. Every so often, I would check in the mornings to see whether any had moved from their spots, for I believed their roots were like legs and feet. And if that were so, couldn't they just pull up root and walk away? Or dance with one another? Was whistling their song part of the dance? Did they stay in the grove, or did they travel across the road to the larger timber and dance with the other trees there?

The nights held mystery for me as a child. I feared the dark, feared what I couldn't see, feared the sounds, the smells. Why did the world change so much when the sun went away, replaced by the moon? Or on a moonless night, replaced by a deep, all-engulfing darkness? For there were no nearby neighbors, and no lights to be seen—I could see nothing outside my bedroom window.

My fears were many. What if the war that was being fought in Korea came to Iowa? Where would we hide? The cellar was cold and damp. And, surely, they would find us there. What would the soldiers do to us? And what if the bombs came? And what of the men who often traveled the roads, the shirts on their backs their only possessions. My mother used to give them a sandwich or two if they found their way down the lane to the house. And she'd wish them better luck than they'd had. Where did they come from and where did they go? Were they still there in the darkness?

When my children were small and were afraid, I remembered how fear often consumed me as a little girl. I could do nothing but listen to them and comfort them as best I could. I asked questions and more questions to make sure they understood that they were safe and able to sleep in peace.

It seemed to have worked. When they grew up, they weren't afraid. And my granddaughter, who also had a fear of the night, was consoled by her parents. I celebrate that the cycle of fear, perhaps generations of fear, has been broken at last.

A STRANGE OLD LADY

A very weird thing has happened. A strange old lady has moved into my house. I have no idea who she is, where she came from, or how she got in. I certainly did not invite her. All I know is that one day, she wasn't there, and the next day she was.

She is a very clever old lady. She manages to keep out of sight for the most part but whenever I pass a mirror I catch a glimpse of her. And whenever I look directly into the mirror to check my appearance there she is, hogging the whole thing and completely obliterating my gorgeous face and body. This is very rude! I have tried screaming at her to stop it, but she just screams back grimacing horribly. She really is quite frightening!

If she insists on hanging around, the least she could do is offer to pay a little rent. But, no! Every once in a while I do find a dollar bill stuck into a coat pocket or some loose change under a sofa cushion but that is not nearly enough. In fact, I don't want to jump to conclusions, but I think she is stealing money from me. I go to the ATM and withdraw $100 and a few days later, it is all gone. I certainly don't spend money that fast, so I can only conclude that the old lady is pilfering from me.

You would think she would use some of that money to buy some wrinkle cream. God knows she needs it! And money isn't the only thing I think she is taking. Food seems to disappear at an alarming rate, too. Especially the good stuff like ice cream, cookies, and candy. I just can't seem to keep that stuff in the house anymore. She really must have a sweet tooth, but she better watch it because she is really packing on the pounds. I think she realizes that, and to make herself feel better, she is tampering with my scale to make me think I am putting on weight too.

For an old lady, she is quite childish though. She likes to play these nasty games, like going into my closet when I'm not home and altering my clothes so they don't fit. Or messing with my files and papers so I can't find them. This is particularly annoying, since I am an extremely neat and organized person. She fiddles with my DVD player to make it not record what I have carefully and correctly programmed it to record.

She has found other imaginative ways to annoy me. She gets to my mail, newspapers and magazines before I do, and somehow blurs the print so badly I can't read it. And she has done something really sinister to the volume control on my TV, radio and telephone so that I hear only mumbles and whispers. She has done other things like make my stairs steeper, my vacuum cleaner heavier, and all my knobs and faucets harder to turn. She even made my bed higher so that getting in and out of bed is a real challenge. Furthermore, she gets to my groceries before I get them put away. I think she puts super glue on the lids of everything, making it almost impossible for me to open them. Is this any way to repay me for letting her stay?

I don't get any respite at night because more than once, her snoring has awakened me. It is very unattractive! And as if that weren't bad enough, she is no longer confining her tactics to the house.

She has found a way to sneak into my car and follow me everywhere I go.

Just when I thought she couldn't get any more cruel, she proved me wrong. She came with me to get my driver's license picture taken, and just as the camera shutter clicked, she jumped in front of me! Who is going to believe that the picture of that old lady is me?

On second thought, maybe I needn't be too hasty. I'll bet I can claim her as a dependent. I'm calling the IRS office tomorrow. Wait! I wonder if she will sabotage that idea too because she always knows what I'm planning and does it first.

Sigh—what's a body to do?

OH, TO BE A CHILD AGAIN

I've been having some double vision for quite a while, making it hard to read. Seeing two or more of the words on a page pretty much messes up any kind of understanding and concentration. My regular ophthalmologist called it "convergence insufficiency" which could apply to many things—for instance, those times when married couples can't quite get on the same page! You know.

Back to my vision: I was referred to a pediatric ophthalmologist whose patients are little kids. Yesterday was the big day. First the forms to fill out online: Patient's name, birthdate, parent signature, no other children from the family allowed in the waiting room, responsible party signature. So I complete these and head out for the exam.

I walk into a waiting room filled with little kids watching *101 Dalmatians* on the TV screen. After signing in, I get a tag with my name, barcode and birthdate, which I stick onto my lapel. What the heck? Do they think I'll forget who I am, or if I get lost, someone will return me to where I am supposed to be? I find a corner where I try to make myself invisible and not have to hear the little ones asking their moms or dads what that grandmother is doing here.

Eventually, the medical assistant comes for me, takes me into the inner offices, points left and says we're going to the blue room. Yada-yada. She finishes all of the intake and leaves. "The doctor will be in shortly," she says.

I hear him with a two-year-old in the next room. The little girl is crying, his voice is consoling. It doesn't take very long and I hear them saying goodbye. The door to the "blue room," my "blue room" opens, and I meet my new doctor. A cordial, very efficient and busy man, we go through the initial questions, and he's ready to take a look at my beautiful green eyes.

He opens this drawer and takes out a little fire engine, about the size of the Hot Wheels cars my kids played with so many years ago. When he points it at my eye, a light goes on, and I realize this is a medical instrument! Okay, so now I am convulsing with laughter. This feels like a cartoon: A doctor is holding a little fire engine with a light that shows what is wrong with my eyes. I'm 79, for God's sakes! He is a pediatric ophthalmologist, and his patients are children, so he uses age-appropriate instruments, he says, "And isn't there a child inside all of us?"

In the end, I walk out with a prescription for prism reading glasses, which I'm told will cost much more than I've ever paid, but I should be able to see clearly the letters on the page again.

Driving home, I tell myself that life is filled with surprises. At least, there was no siren on that little fire engine. Yet, maybe a siren would have amazed and quieted the crying two-year-old. They like that kind of thing.

CHAPTER 12

Walking in the Light

BIRDS, PEACE, GRATITUDE

I wake to the morning stillness. It's been a long, so hot summer. This morning promises coolness, fall is in the air. Fresh, sweet air in the outdoors. Alive with sounds this day, sounds of the early day in the city, sounds of nature. Birds everywhere, the little rabbit dashes from bush to bush, butterflies and all sorts of flying creatures. Even the furry caterpillars have come out.

I hear the birds calling to one another, all kinds, I think. I wish Jim, my husband, were still here. There was a time when he could tell me which sound belonged to each bird. Now I wonder. I wonder about bird sounds and so many other things he knew.

My mind was filled during that time with the passion to make the world a better place. Today, I know I can't do it all, though I still look beyond my home, my safe place and see the problems in the world. I can't help it. It's in my bones to look outward. I ask myself, "Who is my sister? Who is my brother? Is not every living thing precious? My sister? My brother?"

What needs to be protected and what needs to change? What can I do? How can I be a part of that? In the back of my mind, always questioning what it is I am to do. Take it to prayer: "Loving Creator grant me peace, serenity, acceptance, hope, and faith filled with gratitude." For this moment, hear the birds, see the rabbits, follow the butterflies. And all shall, indeed, be well.

ALL OF IT

This window opens
And the world suddenly appears
In all its glory
And imperfection
All of it

The ground is covered with birdseed
Suddenly flocks of doves
Descend from everywhere
Come for the first meal of the day
All of them

Something frightens them
In unison they take to the air
As they fly to safety
Somewhere I cannot go
All of them

Sometimes I want to fly
To a safe place
I look around and I find
It is here, it is home
All of it

THE TREE

A eucalyptus tree stands directly in front of me. I look at this tree with its large, abundant trunk. Three large branches reach to the sky. Anchored to the earth, its roots reach far and deep into the soil where it finds its life nourishment. Standing tall, stately, visible in spite of the fog, its leaves are green and full. This tree is strong, steady, solid and beautiful.

No one tends it, the birds nest in it. Children climb in it and swing from the branches. It gives shade to all who sit beneath it. The angels hover all around.

I want to be the tree. Am I?

IT COULD HAPPEN

I have a vivid imagination—so I'm told. I really don't think it's imagination as much as thinking ahead and being prepared for what could happen. My friend calls it making movies in my head! Take the other day: My son had brought a package of chicken thighs over. He likes the way I bake them, so I fixed them for him to take home. He added them to a bag with other food, and put it on the fireplace hearth.

I should mention that my son's beagle, T3, is living at my house for awhile. If you know beagles, you know they have a nose that can sniff out anything that might taste good. He doesn't miss the tiniest morsel dropped on the floor. More about that later.

I decided to drive my son home, so he packed everything in my little Ford Escape, and off we went! Upon arriving at his apartment, he took his things out. Whoops, no food bag. Oh, no—the chicken thighs were in that bag, and I knew T3 would find them.

I had committed to having dinner with a good friend, so I so put the chicken thighs out of my head for the moment and met her as planned. We had Thai, I ordered #3 spice with tofu. First bite took my breath away, I sent it back for less spice. Thai spice is not like the American Southwestern spice I'm used to! Replacement came: same dish, but fairly tasteless— and made with chicken. Chicken! Darn, I had stopped worrying about what might be happening with the chicken in the bag on my fireplace.

My imagination picked up where I had left off and I just knew T3 had followed his nose to the bag on the fireplace, the scent of the chicken was so enticing he couldn't resist. He had pawed his way through to the package of thighs and had gorged on this wonderful gift that had been left for him. Those were chicken thighs with bones. He had gotten a bone splinter stuck in his throat, had choked and died. What would I tell my son? T3 is his most beloved pal. My son would be so upset that he would never speak to me again.

I went home, prepared to face what I knew I would find. Cautiously opening the door I was met by a happy, healthy beagle. No bag on the fireplace hearth. What the heck! My search began for the missing food bag containing the chicken thighs. Following a logical path and my nose—I can smell out things most other people can't—I found it in the garage, ready to be put into the Escape. This was the middle of summer, so, of course, the temperature in the garage was over 100 degrees. T3 and my son were fine. The only casualty: a package of chicken thighs that found its way to the trash.

Relieved that my imagined scenario hadn't happened, I poured a glass of chardonnay. Still, it could have happened—couldn't it?

HERE ON PALMERSTON ROAD

The minstrel sings on the corner
The seagulls call to one another
There are two different calls
Well, maybe three

The minstrel with his aged voice on the corner
The white gull, whose call is a bit melodic
The gray gull more of a cry
Not dissimilar from that of a child

Each calls to others
In this seaside place
Where people find each other
And others lose each other
Sometimes even themselves

HIS DEMONS

The man who used to live below this window
In a tiny tent next to a wall
He had his demons, as we all do
His were just much more cruel

He would shout out to no one
And everyone
One time he had a knife
He used to stab the invisible ones

Right there under his feet
Striking the cobblestones
Again and again
Screaming senseless sounds

He was feared by some
Tourists stared
Keeping distance
Wondering

Locals walked by
Sometimes left food
Or a blanket, a sweater
He belonged to them

The police would take him away
Only to bring him back a few days later
He lived in that tiny tent
With his demons

Two mornings ago they came again
The tent and he are gone

SAY HELLO, SAY GOODBYE

Life continues
As it was

Doesn't anyone know
A star flickered
And died last night?
And now the night will be
A little less bright?

Didn't anyone see
The star's last brilliant
Flight as it fell from
Its place in the vast night sky?

Doesn't anyone care about
The death of a love
That no one knew about?
And isn't the world less
Without that precious love?

HOPE

Hope is that part of us
That knows all is
As it should be
It is the underpinnings
Of the joy a well-lived life brings

Hope is not pretending
That troubles don't exist
It is the trust
That they will not last forever
That hurts will be healed
And difficulties overcome

It is faith
That a source of strength and renewal
Lies within
To lead us through the dark
To the sunshine
One more time

THE VISITOR

What is it?
Who is it?
Someone with answers?
Someone expected?

Check every room
Every closet
Look under each bed
Careful now

Still no one
Nothing
Wait!
Come in

Welcome
Sit down
Tell me, tell me
What I must know

Listen and remember
There is love here
It is safe here
Peace lives here

My blessing I leave
For you, for your home
For all who enter here
Farewell

Farewell
Thank you
Safe travels to you
Unknown Visitor

REMEMBERING

Remembering
Always remembering
Memories
So long ago

Not so long ago
Perception
Perspective
Missing

New freedom
To explore
To go
To be

Whoever
Whatever
Wherever
Whenever

ON A SILENT RETREAT

There is a fountain here
Water gushes and splatters
Making rainbows in the noontime sun
And cooling me as I walk by

Beauty blooms around it
Today visited by butterflies
Yellow ones, orange ones
All flitting from blossom to blossom

All gathering nectar
Here in this place where all are fed
All are nourished
All spirits are renewed

This place where peace abides
Left by those who came before
Footprints in sand and on rocks
Left their mark, as we leave ours

Who has been here before
A crowd, a single person
No matter, we are all one
Belonging to one another

Creating a pastoral print
Of many colors
Blended, as with watercolors
Brushed onto blank papers

Each color blending into the next
Creating new colors
Some beautiful, some strange
But blending all the same

A masterpiece, a kaleidoscope
Ever-changing
Always beautiful
We are one

HOME

How far do we have to go
To be safe, happy, at home
Look into your heart
That is home

You are home
Wherever you are
Home is nowhere
And everywhere

FROM LIGHT TO DARKNESS TO LIGHT

For so many years, I've walked in the light. It is safe, with illuminated pathways all around. It was probably in my teen years when I found solid ground and felt there might be a particular path for me. It was easy to take the path I thought was meant for me, and I gladly stepped onto the pathway and then discovered, that, no, there really was none. I had to tread lightly to find my way, to make my own path. Knowing we never walk alone, I grabbed hold of the Spirit's hand and walked on.

One hand firmly held by Spirit, the other empty, I reached out and found my partner-love-husband. Now accompanied by my travel companions, my path was more defined. The path, smooth, winding, sometimes blocked by stones, brought me to a looming darkness ahead. My earthly companion couldn't stay. Illness ended our partnership, leaving one hand empty, cold, almost lifeless.

My other hand remained in the hand of the Spirit, who would never let go and carried me when I couldn't walk on my own. Always there, always.

Ahead was only darkness—ominous, feared—no one goes there alone. They would be consumed and become a part of it. I fiercely resisted. I don't want to go there. I am afraid, I don't know what will happen, where I will be. Where is the path? I cannot see. No, I am not going.

My only companion, the one who has been with me since before I came into this human form, reaches out but I don't see. Out of desperation and sheer fear

I listen, for that is all I can do. I listen for signs of this Spirit in the breeze rustling the palm leaves outside the window, in the never-ending waves of the ocean that relentlessly pound the beach, the ebb and flow of the universe, of life itself.

I hear the sounds of the birds, the ocean birds, the rumble in the storm clouds as they form in the vast blue-gray sky which meets the ocean in the far distance. The clouds now release the rain and I hear the ping-ping increase to a steady pounding on the roof. The storm passes.

It is silent now. A small voice comes from somewhere? With a simple message, "I am here, I have always been here. I will always be here. You are My daughter, the very essence of Me, how could I abandon you? Yes, the darkness looms directly in front of us. You must walk into it, you must in order to find the new light that your life will be, now that your earthly companion is gone. There is no choice if you want to live. If you choose to not go, you perish. I don't want that. You may want that right now—but you must take my hand and walk into the darkness in search of a new path. It will reveal itself as you walk, one step, even if a reluctant one, one step at a time.

"It can be a trying journey: pack simply, travel light, you won't need much, a backpack, maybe. We will walk together, it is a promise. I will not lose you, you will not get lost, trust Me because you are Me and I am you. No greater love is there than the love of the Creator for the created one. We are one."

Come now, let us begin again.

AFTERWORD

In tribute to my husband Jim, I wanted to share the eulogy that my son, Chris, wrote for Jim's memorial service. He so beautifully describes his dad and their relationship. Mike, my other son, would tell you about the times he spent with his dad in much the same way. I have always been grateful for their love of one another. Read on. —*Bonnie*

EULOGY FOR JIM DANOWSKI
by Chris Danowski

Thank you for coming today. I want to talk to you about my dad. While I would love to tell you lots of stories about him that have nothing to do with his illness, I think it's either impossible, or maybe unnecessary, to try. It's not that he was his illness. But illness was one of the great running themes through his whole life. The radical spirituality that my dad had, one that evolved through his life, came through his experiences with pain, or, sometimes, in spite of the pain.

The other great thread that runs through his life, of course, is his love for my mother. His story really is a love story. So. I want to talk about pain and I want to talk about love.

First, there's insomnia. When I was a little kid, sometimes I had nightmares or just couldn't sleep, so I'd get up and go out in the living room. He was almost always awake pretty late in those days, dealing with his pain during the first years of his Multiple Sclerosis. On some nights, we'd watch *Benny Hill*, *Monty Python*, *Saturday Night Live*, and *SCTV*. Other nights I'd ask him to tell me stories about his own childhood, when he was a boy growing up in Wisconsin.

He'd talk about the family farm, the tavern that my grandparents ran, stories about my aunts and uncles. Sometimes he'd talk about the Air Force. Men banded together and living underground in Alaska, building radio tubes for NASA, and men going crazy from the cold and the isolation, or the relentless dark, or the relentless light, watching TV when the tv wasn't on. And men cracking jokes, trying to find ways to have fun in spite of their situation.

For awhile, in Alaska, he was working as a DJ. There were times when they were required to maintain Radio Silence. The air would be quiet, absolutely quiet, while all the men on headphones would be listening to each other, listening to each other staying quiet. Eventually, someone would whisper, "Who dat?" And after a few moments, someone else would whisper, "Who dat? Who dat do dat?" And the superior officer would burst in and yell at everyone, "This is radio silence!" and it would be quiet again for a while. Then, "Who dat?" "Who dat do dat?"

It might come as a shock to some of you, but my dad wasn't terribly fond of authority. When I was trying to be a hippie when I was 16, I asked for his old military gear so I could wear it and pretend I was John Lennon. He told me it was long gone, all that stuff. He'd thrown it away, disgusted with the whole thing.

But oddly, he always had a respect for the kind of authority that people earn through serving a higher good. He always has had a great love for this place, and felt lucky to be here. And he taught me that the only thing to do with this feeling of luck was to show gratitude by working to make things better, especially for those who were in situations where the odds were stacked against them. I'll talk about that in just a minute. But I want to tell this one story, about his respect for authority, that took me by surprise. This was in June, this year. He had had a serious infection after the last surgery, and wasn't in a very good state. He was hallucinating pools filled with puppies at the nurse's station, and told me that I needed to call the police right away, because the people in the hospital were doing experiments on him. He said he'd had some bizarre treatments in the Air Force in the late 1950s, and no doubt he was convinced this was happening to him again. He asked me to get his clothes together, because we were going to bust out of the hospital. He got quiet. He heard the nurses outside the door. And he said, in a very loud voice, "I would like to request a leave of absence."

I like to think this is just a leave of absence.

My dad was a mystic. When he was young, he wanted to be a saint, and do the things that matter in this world. During our late night talks, he would sometimes tell me about these intense spiritual experiences. His internal world, especially his world of dreams, was just as real as his waking experiences. I have a wanderlust, a terrible wanderlust, and I get that from him, but his wanderlust was on a more spiritual realm. His soul was always traveling, and he never seemed to need to go anywhere else. But he liked hearing about my travels in the world as much as I liked his stories about traveling in spirit worlds.

When I was a teenager, he changed. He decided to stop taking so many pain pills, because he didn't like how they changed his mood so much. My mom told us that he was doing this because he wanted to be a better father. He and my mom both started meditating together more often.

There were lots of mornings, coming into the living room, they would be sitting quietly together. Um. Ok. Sometimes his meditation included sounds, sounds that were a lot like snoring. Dreaming is meditating, too. It counts.

My favorite stories are love stories, and the one between my mother and father is the one that started it all for me. Here's a bit of their song, the one they first heard when they were setting out on their honeymoon, driving from Phoenix to up North, "In the Misty Moonlight."

I learned from my dad that great love is fueled by a sense of adventure, and we get to wake up and find ourselves connected to something larger than ourselves. I got to know this early on, and I got to have love and adventure blend together in my life. I had a lot of adventures with Tamara, when we were married, and our daughter, Elli, seems to get it, too. I'm really terribly grateful that we all live close together, so these relationships could continue. I know he loved you both dearly, and I also know that you know that, too.

The spiritual sustenance that my parents gave to each other was never an escape from the world, or a retreat; quite the opposite, it was the very thing that made action in the world possible.

My parents met in the middle of the civil rights movement, and anti-war activism. My dad told me lots of stories about brushes with FBI agents, or other suspected members of certain intelligence organizations. They tried to get him to join intelligence in the military, and it almost seemed as though they'd been following him ever since. He really seemed to kind of like the idea that they were keeping tabs on him, that this meant that he was, indeed, living a life where he was doing things that matter.

My mom is also one of those people who has given her life to doing things that matter. It's her life work. And my dad never considered this only her work, it was theirs. She was the foot soldier, out in the fields, getting arrested, and meeting people like Cesar Chavez and Martin Sheen. Even though he wasn't necessarily there physically, he was there with her, always right there.

She really is his everything. She was the touchstone for his deep meditation experiences, the one who was walking the footsteps of Martin Luther King and Gandhi for them, and she was the muse, the one for whom he sang.

Their relationship never stopped evolving. When they started praying together more often, they developed their own language, their own shorthand, and in the last years, it was always a little spooky how little they would say to each other in order to understand each other completely.

When we were all together in the hospital last fall, after he fell and broke his shoulder, the nurse call button was broken. The technicians were in a number of times. They couldn't get the call button to work (which, really, is a little alarming, because you might think that of all the complicated machines there, the call button wouldn't pose such a threat), so they gave him a bell. So he would ring the bell and they still wouldn't hear it, so my mom would go get their attention.

During the last months, when he was home in bed, he developed his own call button, one vastly superior to the hospital bell technology: a T-bone doggie toy. Growing up poor, along with experience in broken situations in the military, you have to use your own wits and develop your own technologies. He would squeak the toy to get the attention of Mike and my mom, and they would come.

I have another relic of my dad's communication technologies. My phone died last week, so I'm using his old phone. This one has some of their old text messages to each other, and I've been able to read some very touching exchanges, like this, where he writes, "Where's the cash, need to pay the hooker," and she writes, "You are a veteran, tell her it is a service to her country."

I'm sorry I missed one of the last months, I was away in Berlin. I wasn't really sure I should even go, when it started to seem like the timing might be too close. But—my dad told me, "You're happy when you're traveling, you're happy when you're going somewhere else, you're happy when you're in strange cities having adventures. You shouldn't settle anywhere. The most important thing is that you have fun."

The day before I left, I met up with an acquaintance, and I expected to have coffee, and I didn't expect to fall in love, but I got both. So while I was having an adventure in Berlin, my head was there, but my heart was back here. I went to sleep, and I woke up, wondering about Heather, and worrying about my dad. It was beautiful and painful all at the same time. Just a few weeks later, these worlds came together. One night, Heather came over to meet the parents, and when she started rubbing my dad's feet, I couldn't help but think something mythic might be going on. And I don't think it's too far out there to consider that this is all part of a greater design, that this experience of pain and beauty brought me closer to my dad, so I could understand just a little bit of what it's like to live in his life. Everything that's important, that matters, that's dear to me, is all very apparent, right there on the surface, and everything else just doesn't matter.

We all knew the time was coming, but I think everyone was surprised at how quick it was. I know he had to go, but I really wanted him to be around longer, even just a little bit longer. One time, we were talking on the phone, and I was telling him how I would be coming home for a visit after a long time away. He said, "It'll be so nice to have you sitting here next to me again, just watching TV." I know how he feels. I'd like that, too. I'm a little mad we never got to have a last, long conversation, but I'll get over it. I can talk to him now, and I can hear him talking back to me. There's always more to say, the conversation isn't over.

When I got back from Berlin, I got to see how much he depended on my brother, Mike, and my mother to make his days peaceful, and full of wild, romantic dreams, the kind of thing a beautiful life is built on. And in the very last days, visitors in person, visitors by phone, I saw love in action, and how love makes us do beautiful things when we are breaking. I do think this is a beautiful end of just one chapter in his love story. We get born and take our first breath, and at the very end, it's back to the breath. One last breath, and we leave the body behind, sometimes, if we're lucky, with a mad and beautiful grin.

Thanks, Dad.

Bonnie & Jim

ABOUT THE AUTHOR

Bonnie Goldsmith Danowski is a lifelong innovator, writer, teacher and advocate for society's most vulnerable: those at the beginning, at the end, and in the shadows of life. She has served on various national, state and local councils, boards and committees. She has presented papers at conferences and other gatherings referencing health care, equality, caregiving, and advocacy. She has testified before congressional and state committees, and spoken with members of the U.S. Congress, Arizona Legislature, other elected officials and collaborating organizations.

As the primary caregiver for her husband, Jim, from the time he was diagnosed with multiple sclerosis in 1971 until his death in 2013, Bonnie speaks passionately both from understanding the issues and her own lived experience. She is the primary advocate for her son, who has a bipolar/ co-occuring disability.

Bonnie has received numerous awards and recognition for her advocacy work. These include being co-founder of the Phoenix Catholic Diocese Desert Pilgrims for those with disabilities 1978; Fearless Caregiver Magazine Care Hero 2003; AZ Chapter of Paralyzed Veterans of America President's Award 2004; AZ Chapter of the MS Society Advocate of the Year 2005 and 2015; National MS Society Advocacy Hall of Fame 2012; ARCH National Respite Coalition Advocate 2009; and Phoenix Catholic Diocese Lifetime Achievement Award 2007. In 2011, she was given the "Bonnie" Award for Advocate of the Year by the AZ Caregiver Coalition. She has worked closely with

American Association of Retired People (AARP), Area Agencies on Aging, interfaith councils, and other non-governmental organizations. Bonnie is a Valley Interfaith Project founding co-chair, co-founder of the AZ Caregiver Coalition, and former committee member of the City of Phoenix Disability Office.

In 2007, while a leader in Valley Interfaith Project, she co-wrote legislation which instituted the Lifespan Respite Care Act, continuing to provide respite to hundreds of family caregivers over the years.

Bonnie is a Reiki Practitioner, and for fun loves to bead, paint (a little) and learn new things.

Bonnie Goldsmith
Danowski

Made in the USA
Middletown, DE
18 April 2022

64342398R00169